This book is from
the kitchen library of

_____

Mr. Food®
Pizza 1-2-3

Art Ginsburg
Mr. Food®

WILLIAM MORROW AND COMPANY, INC.

New York

Library of Congress Cataloging-in-Publication Data
Ginsburg, Art.
  Mr. Food®: pizza 1-2-3 / Art Ginsburg.—1st ed.
    p.   cm.
  Includes index.
  ISBN 0–688–14417–9
  1. Pizza.   I. Title: Mister Food®: pizza 1-2-3.
TX770.P58G55   1996
641.8'24—dc20   95–41522
                                                                          CIP

Printed in the United States of America

First Edition

1   2   3   4   5   6   7   8   9   10

BOOK DESIGN BY MICHAEL MENDELSOHN OF MM DESIGN 2000, INC.

Dedicated to
All my buddies
who shared countless pizzas with me in the primo pizzerias of
Troy, Albany, and Schenectady, New York.
Those sure were great times and great tastes!

Acknowledgments

Writing a book is something like making a pizza—you have to have good solid groundwork and build from there. If I had to compare my staff with a pizza, it'd go something like this:

The crust, my foundation, is Ethel and the rest of my family, and also my creative kitchen staff—Joe Peppi, Patty Rosenthal, Alice Palombo, Janice Bruce, and Mike Arnaud.

On top of the crust is the sauce—that's where my administrative and office staff fit in. Steve and Chuck Ginsburg, Laura Ratcliff, Marilyn Ruderman, Beth Ives, Stacey Dempsey, Tom Palombo, and Mark Hayward...they're quite a saucy crew!

And who wants a pizza without toppings?! I've got just the right combination with a little of this and a little of that from Al Marchioni and the super group at William Morrow, including my enthusiastic new editor, Zachary Schisgal, and the talented Richard Aquan. Skip Dye and Deborah Weiss Geline add just the right amount of pizzazz to the mix.

I couldn't forget the spicing done by Bill Adler, Phyllis Heller, Michael Mendelsohn, and Roy Fantel.

Mostly there's the cheese—the ingredient that holds it all together. And this pizza has two people, or shall I say, "big cheeses," who kept all the ingredients blending well: Caryl Ginsburg Fantel and Howard Rosenthal. These two definitely do not melt in the heat!

I'm grateful to all of them, as well as to all of my enthusiastic viewers and readers, and to the following companies and organizations that help make *this* pizza more than just your average pizza:

M. E. Heuck Co., makers of Firm Grip™ kitchen tools
Dairy Management Inc.
Tryson House, makers of flavor sprays
Jana Brands, makers of frozen seafood products
Villa Valenti Classic Sauce Company
Boboli®, makers of shelf-stable prepared pizza shells

Contents

Introduction

Almost everybody loves *some* kind of pizza—and people are usually very particular about *how* they like it. Some like thick crust, others thin, and still others prefer deep-dish. Some like it simple with just cheese and tomato sauce and others want it smothered with toppings. And for many of us, having pizza is as simple as calling the local pizzeria and ordering our favorite kind.

But there's nothing like homemade pizza right out of the oven, prepared just the way you like it, and anyone who's made it at home knows it's simple to make...really! The recipes in this book are all easy to make, because I've given you lots of options. If you want to do it all the way, you can start with your own dough made from scratch. I've got some great dough recipes for you—and even some super variations for those, too, like Cheesy Crust Dough (page 8), and Crushed Red Pepper Dough (page 5) and Cornmeal Dough (page 5). But if you'd prefer to start with premade dough or a prepared pizza shell, that's fine, too—it sure is easier! And you can use prepared sauces—from tomato to pesto and more—or make your own quick sauces. ("No Time" Homemade Pizza Sauce, page 16, doesn't even need to be cooked!) There are so many pizza dough and sauce choices available to us these days! You can find more about them in the first chapter, **The Building Blocks: Doughs and Sauces**.

As far as we can tell, the first pizzas were made and eaten in Naples, Italy, in the late 1700s. There have been tons of pizza variations since then (with lots more to come, I'm sure!), but I've got some of the traditional favorites in the second chapter. From No-Rules Cheese Pizza (page 24) to White Pizza (page 29), Meatball Pizza (page 37), and Chicago Deep-Dish Sausage Pizza (page 39), these are all sure winners. (And you can create your own traditional signature pizzas by mixing and matching toppings—check out my list of Toppings for Cheese Pizza on page 25.)

Even though pizza originated in Italy, today we can enjoy it with the taste influences of many other cultures. Go ahead and take a trip around the world with Teriyaki Chicken Pizza (page 49), Chicken Fajita Pizza (page 52), Fish 'n' Chips Pizza (page 62), Israeli Pizza (page 63), and more that are really out of this world!

After you return from your taste trip around the world, you'll be ready for taste adventures with pizzas that are a bit unusual. In **Not-Your-Average Pizzas** I've got treats that are bound to become family and entertaining favorites. There's Chicken and Roasted Garlic Pizza (page 82), Crabmeat and Pesto Pizza (page 87), Omelet "Pizza" (page 76), and Spicy Mushroom Pizza (page 101).

We often see **Stuffed Pizzas and Calzones** at pizzerias. These are heartier versions of pizza, and they're pretty easy to make at home, too. With fillings like ham and Swiss cheese (page 121), spinach and ricotta cheese (page 116), and Sloppy Joes (page 110), there are lots of choices. Why, there's even a Shepherd's Pie Pizza here (page 113)!

Did you ever think of making pizza with sandwich fillings? Why not?! In **Pizzas That Think They're Sandwiches**, you'll see how perfectly some of our favorite sandwich ingredients top pizzas! So, the next time the gang comes over for dinner, serve Cheeseburger Pizza (page 130); for brunch, surprise them with Lox, Cream Cheese, and Onion Pizza (page 137); and for lunch, serve Turkey Club Pizza (page 134)—and don't forget the pickles!

Most of the pizzas in here are pretty quick, but for those times when you've got to have something super-fast, make **Presto Pizzas!** These are creative pizzas made on bases of English muffins, bagels, flour tortillas, refrigerated biscuits, pita bread, or French bread.

And, speaking of bread, a pizza cookbook wouldn't be complete without focaccia, bruschetta, and other Italian breads. After all, as the story goes, pizza actually started as a snack for Italian women while they waited for their bread to bake in their town's communal ovens. They'd simply break off a piece of the bread dough, flatten it, and top it with whatever seasonings they had on hand. It baked quickly, without tomato sauce *or* cheese. So, not only do I have a selection of tasty **Simple Italian Breads** like Herb Focaccia (page 166), Classic Bruschetta (page 162), and Tangy Bread Sticks (page 170), but I've even included tips for making Flavored Butters (page 171) and Flavored Oils (page 172) that are perfect spreading and dipping partners for these breads.

The first American pizzeria opened in New York City in 1905, but pizza didn't catch on outside our Italian neighborhoods until after World War II, when American soldiers returned from duty in Italy and insisted on introducing it to their families and friends. Those pizzas were mostly the mozzarella cheese and tomato variety, certainly not dessert pizzas! But after you've tried a selection of traditional and unusual pizzas and Italian breads, you've got to try some **Dessert Pizzas**. And I've got a selection that should satisfy any sweet tooth—from Fruity Pizza (page 176) and Black Forest Pizza (page 181) to Apple Crumb Pizza (page 183) and Lemon Meringue Pizza (page 189). Surprised? Wait till you taste them!

Now that you've gotten a hint of what's ahead, I bet you're ready to start turning your kitchen into the best and busiest pizzeria in the neighborhood!

Have fun...I know you're in for lots of

"OOH IT'S SO GOOD!!™"

Pizza Pointers

Handy Kitchen Helpers

Making pizza really is easy, and it should be fun, too. Other than this book, you shouldn't need any equipment other than what's already in your kitchen and pantry. But in case you want to go a bit further, I'm going to tell you about some equipment that can make your pizza-making experience a breeze:

- **Baker's peel:** A paddle-shaped tool made of metal or wood that is used to slide pizza onto and off a pizza baking stone or tile. The front edge is beveled to make the movement easier.
- **Dry measuring cups:** Available in $1/4$-cup, $1/3$-cup, $1/2$-cup, and 1-cup measurements, for dry ingredients. Easy to level. Usually made of plastic or metal.
- **Electric mixer:** There are two basic varieties: the portable hand-held type, ideal for cookies and light tasks, and the standing tabletop type, ideal for larger jobs and quantities.

- **Food processor:** Here's a piece of equipment that's not required for pizza-making, but it sure does help cut down on preparation time. There are many brands available, but I recommend one with a highly efficient motor that will hold up to the demanding task of mixing and kneading pizza dough; it should also have a large-capacity bowl. For pizza-making, the best type is one that comes with a selection of attachments, such as a steel cutting blade (which is just great for making dough) and a grating/shredding blade. Don't forget to make certain that cleanup is easy, 'cause if something isn't easy, it isn't a timesaver.
- **Glass measuring cups:** Most commonly available in 1-cup, 2-cup, and 4-cup sizes. Ideal for liquid measures.
- **Kitchen shears or scissors:** A great option for cutting pizza (instead of using a pizza wheel). Just snip and enjoy. If you have these, make sure to keep them for food use *only*.
- **Knives:** A sharp serrated (waved-edge) knife is perfect for cutting breads and works well on pizzas, too, instead of a pizza wheel. A paring knife is just right for smaller jobs because it gives a greater feeling of control.
- **Measuring spoons:** Available in sets that include ¼-teaspoon, ½-teaspoon, 1-teaspoon, and 1-tablespoon measurements. Some sets also include a ⅛-teaspoon size. Usually made of plastic or metal and often connected on a ring for convenience.
- **Mixing bowls:** The basics of any kitchen. Made of stainless steel, glass, plastic, or earthenware, and usually graduated in size. It's good to have at least one full set.
- **Mixing spoons:** You probably have a drawerful of wooden, plastic, or metal mixing spoons in a wide variety of sizes. Unless a recipe specifies, the choice is yours.
- **Oven thermometer:** To make a great pizza, you must bake it in a very hot oven. Make sure yours is properly calibrated so that you're sure you're baking at the proper temperature. You can check your oven's calibration with an inexpensive oven thermometer. (Be careful when removing your thermometer from the oven, because it will be very hot!)

- **Pizza pans and baking surfaces:** *Traditional pizza pan:* A 6- to 14-inch round pan made of metal (which, incidentally, is a great conductor of heat). Many are available with nonstick finishes; that really helps with cleanup! I suggest using a high-quality pan because you'll want one that won't warp under high oven temperatures. *Pizza crisping pan:* The perfect pan for baking or reheating pizza. Similar to a traditional pizza pan, but with perforations that allow hot air to circulate through the pan to crisp the dough as the pizza bakes. *Cookie sheet:* Yup, the old standby that we use for cookies also works well for pizza. It's rectangular-shaped, available with or without a rimmed edge, and in various finishes, including my favorite: nonstick. *Deep-dish pizza pan:* A metal 10- to 14-inch round deep-dish pizza pan is the ideal pan for deep-dish pizza. The 2-inch-high rim supports the sides of a deep-dish pie. When using hearty toppings, it's best to use a deep-dish pan (and a dough recommended for deep-dish pizzas). A 10- to 14-inch round cake pan will work if a deep-dish pan is not available. *Pizza screen:* This is an open screen supported by a metal ring about 14 inches in diameter. The screen should be coated with nonstick vegetable spray. The pizza is placed right on it and baked; because the screen is so open, the crust has the chance to get nice and crisp while baking. *Pizza baking stone:* A pizza stone is for the "serious" pizza-maker. Made of clay, it can be found in many sizes and various shapes—round, square, or rectangular—and is designed to replicate the high heat of a professional pizza oven. Here's how it works: The stone is placed on the bottom rack of the oven and the oven is preheated for 45 to 50 minutes so the stone absorbs the heat. Then you bake the pizza right on the stone and it creates a crispy crust, just like you get from pizza made in professional pizza ovens. Leave the stone in the oven until completely cooled. Cleanup is a snap; follow the manufacturer's instructions. *Pizza baking tiles:* These are a set of 6 to 8 terra-cotta tiles that sit on a metal tray. The pizza is baked directly on the tiles, creating a crispy crust. The tiles need to be preheated in the oven the same way as a pizza stone.

- **Pizza server or pointed spatula:** A wedge-shaped spatula used for serving pizza slices or wedges.
- **Pizza wheel:** If you don't have one of these, now's the time to get one. Designed to roll and cut at the same time, these make cutting through pizza crust—and toppings—a snap. (After all, this is how they cut pizza in pizzerias, and they must know how well these work!)
- **Portable pizza oven:** If you're really serious about pizza-making, you'll want to check out the many types of portable pizza ovens that are now available in housewares stores and department stores. It's a super option when you want to make a quick pizza without turning on your regular oven.
- **Pot holders:** Available in mitten or pad types. A must for safe cooking, especially since pizza needs to be cooked at such high temperatures.
- **Rolling pin:** Wooden, metal, and marble rolling pins are available for rolling out pizza dough. The surface of a rolling pin must be kept clean and free of dents and nicks. When using it, keep your rolling pin lightly floured to prevent dough from sticking.
- **Rubber spatula:** A helpful utensil for scraping down mixing bowls and for combining ingredients. Sizes and shapes vary. Choose a strong one for mixing and a lighter one for spreading sauces over dough.
- **Saucepans and skillets:** An assortment of sizes is recommended. It's important to have snug-fitting covers for your skillets.
- **Shredder/grater:** These come in several styles and are needed for shredding all types of cheese for pizza. There are also shredding and grating attachments available for food processors. Freshly grated cheese is very flavorful; it's also much more economical to do it yourself.
- **Sifter:** Not a necessity, but still helpful for removing lumps from flour and for mixing dry ingredients. Always make certain that a sifter is completely dry before using.

- **Timer:** A must for worry-free pizza-making. Available in many shapes, sizes, and colors, portable, digital, or even built into your oven.

Now you're probably wondering, "Where do I find all of these basics?" With pizza-making so popular today, many large department stores carry these items along with other kitchen specialty items. (Gourmet kitchen equipment stores generally carry an expanded selection.) Use what you've got on hand, or treat yourself to some new pizza equipment...but go ahead and turn your kitchen into a pizzeria!

Tips for Making, Shaping, and Baking Dough

1. Most of my recipes call for all-purpose flour. You can usually substitute whole wheat flour or another type of flour (except self-rising) in its place. And with today's milling processes, these usually don't need to be sifted.

2. Patience is the key to making good pizza dough. Homemade dough needs time to proof, so, while you're waiting, you can prepare your toppings. That'll help cut down on preparation time.

3. Dough can easily be made in double batches. Why would you want to do that? To save time! Make one for now and one to freeze for the next time you make pizza. Just wrap it well in plastic wrap or a plastic storage bag. Allow it to defrost at room temperature for several hours, or for 24 hours in the refrigerator, before using.

4. When a recipe calls for allowing dough to rise at room temperature, this usually means a temperature between 65° F. and 80°F. The warmer the room, the quicker the dough will rise.

5. "Kneading dough" is a process that can be done by hand or in a food processor (see Traditional Pizza Dough, page 3). The dough is pressed and folded over itself repeatedly until it develops an elastic texture. The finished kneaded dough should be satiny smooth and have an elastic feel, so that it gives structure to the finished crust.

KNEADING DOUGH

Hey! I need dough!

6. "Rising" or "proofing" is the process that occurs when the gases in the dough formed by the yeast cause the dough to increase to as much as double its size. Watch as the dough proofs, and you can actually see it slowly grow!

7. "Punching down": Forget the boxing gloves! This is simply the process of distributing the gases that are formed in the dough during the rising. This can be done by gently pressing down on the dough with the heel of your hand or your fist—that's how it gets its name!

PUNCHING DOWN

Ouch!

8. You must preheat your oven. A hot oven (400°F. to 450°F. for most pizzas) is the key to success for pizza-baking. After all, you want crisp, browned crusts with toppings that are piping hot but not burned. Use an oven thermometer (page xv) to make sure that your oven is properly calibrated.

9. If using a pizza stone or pizza tiles (page xvi), preheat them in the oven on the lowest rack so that you'll produce the hottest possible surface for cooking your pizza. Shape the dough on a baker's peel that has been lightly dusted with cornmeal or flour. Then top it and slide it onto your preheated stone or tiles to bake. When done, remove the pizza with the baker's peel and cut on a cutting board.

10. It's time to shape up—the dough, I mean! In most of my recipes, I suggest spreading the dough out on a 12- to 14-inch

round pizza pan, but there are no rules. Almost any shape or size will work well. Make a diamond shape, a star, or the ever-popular rectangle. (That's actually more Sicilian.) But remember, the odder the shape, the more difficult the pizza will be to handle.

SPREADING DOUGH

Ahh! A MASSAGE!

11. If you want to make individual pizzas, that's no problem. Just cut the dough into smaller portions and shape them as directed.

12. Crust thickness can vary. The choice is yours: A ½-inch-thick dough will bake up soft and chewy, while a ¼-inch-thick dough will yield a crisp crust. Generally, to make a thicker crust using the same amount of dough, you can just spread the dough out into a smaller circle than the recipe specifies. To make a thinner crust, you can just spread the dough out larger.

13. Make an edge on your pizza dough by pinching or fluting the dough with your fingers. Make it high or low, fancy or plain, depending on your toppings.

14. Don't overdo your toppings! Too much topping doesn't give you a better pizza—just a messy, undercooked pizza.

15. To check your pizza for doneness, use a metal spatula to lift up the dough and look underneath. It's done when the bottom of the crust is golden. Be careful—it will be hot!

16. I don't recommend cutting your pizza on its baking pan. It will harm the pan's finish and eventually ruin the pan. Just slide the pizza off its pan onto a cutting board and cut it with a pizza

wheel, serrated knife, or kitchen shears. (See my Pizza-Cutting Guide, page xxiv.)

Which Cheese to Choose

We all know how important cheese is to pizza. After all, it's one of the staples on today's American pizzas. Mozzarella has traditionally been the most common pizza cheese, but lately I've been getting more and more questions about other cheeses that could go on pizzas. And our cheese choices go beyond type and brand! Cheeses are available in so many different forms, too, from block to shredded, grated, sliced, or even crumbled, to seasoned cheese blends. So here's a list of cheese possibilities for pizzas, calzones, and stuffed pizzas, along with a brief description of each. Try some new ones—or mix and match them! Just be sure to sprinkle whatever cheese you use evenly over the entire pizza, or maybe a bit heavier on the outer rim. (That's because during baking, the cheese tends to slide toward the center.) Use your favorites and you'll create your own all-new **"OOH IT'S SO GOOD!!™"**

- **Blue cheese:** A sharp, full-flavored, blue-veined cheese with a crumbly texture. Melts well.
- **Cheddar:** A popular firm cheese available in strengths from mild to extra sharp. Slice or shred it sparingly onto the prepared dough, along with your other cheese(s).
- **Feta cheese:** Traditionally associated with Mediterranean foods, now it is also produced in the United States. Great for crumbling on prepared pizza dough.
- **Fresh or Buffalo mozzarella:** A soft, extremely mild white cheese. It is usually stored and sold in water in order to maintain its pliability. Fresh mozzarella melts easily, so it can be used in slices or chunks on a prepared dough.

- **Goat cheese:** A tangy cheese that melts easily, it is produced from goat's milk and can be crumbled on prepared dough.
- **Havarti:** A mild block cheese with tiny holes and a great texture for melting. Often sold flavored with herbs such as dill and basil.
- **Monterey Jack:** A mild, white cheese that melts easily. Also called Jack cheese, it's quite popular today, both plain and studded with chopped jalapeño peppers (which give a pizza a nice spicy flavor).
- **Mozzarella:** A firm, unripened traditional Italian cheese. Probably the most popular pizza cheese, this is the one most often found packaged in supermarkets. It has a creamy texture, mild flavor, and melts easily.
- **Parmesan:** A very hard Italian cheese available fresh in chunks or grated and shredded in packages. When used on pizza, it's typically an accent to complement other cheeses.
- **Provolone:** A firm, mild white Italian cheese that is slightly smoked and is known for its round shape and medium-soft texture.
- **Ricotta:** A mild-flavored, spreadable white Italian cheese ideal for stuffed pizza and calzones, as well as a rich, fresh-tasting pizza topping.
- **Romano:** A very hard Italian cheese similar to Parmesan and often blended with it.
- **Swiss:** A firm block cheese identifiable by its large holes. Although not a popular pizza cheese, it can add unique flavor to your specialty pizzas. May be sliced or shredded for use on prepared pizza dough.

Pizza-Cutting Guide

Sure, everybody has his or her own way of cutting pizza. But there are variations, and I've got a few pointers and sketches that might help. Choose the method that works best for you.

1. I call this the "pie wedge."

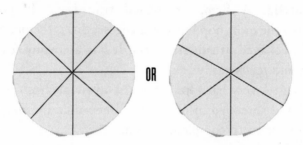

2. And here's the "criss-cross." This is easier to eat, so it's perfect for hors d'oeuvres or those times when you want to sample different pizzas. It's also ideal for the kids.

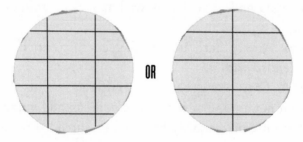

3. The "tic-tac-toe" works with square and rectangular pizzas.

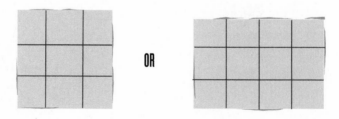

4. To serve a calzone:

Leave whole   **OR**   cut into slices.

5. Give individual pizzas and Presto Pizzas "the old one-two," or serve cut into quarters or left whole.

Cut in half   Cut into quarters   Uncut

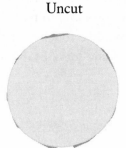

Cutting Tips

1. Choose a pizza wheel (page xvii), kitchen shears or scissors (page xv), or a serrated knife (page xv) for cutting. Be careful to cut your pizza, not your fingers!
2. Always cut on a cutting board. Do not cut pizza on the pizza baking pan, tiles, or stones, as that will damage the finish, and your knife or pizza wheel.
3. Always use quick, firm strokes that go all the way through the toppings and the crust.
4. Since most pizzas are served hot, be careful not to burn yourself when cutting and handling pizza.
5. If you'd like, serve on a clean pizza pan that you reserve just for serving.

Notes from **Mr. Food**®

Lighten Up . . . with Food Sprays

Throughout this book, and in my other cookbooks, I frequently mention nonstick vegetable and baking sprays and recommend using them to coat pans before placing food on them. Here's why—these sprays are easy to use, they add no measurable amount of fat to our food (if used as directed), and now they're even available in non-aerosol *and* in flavored varieties! The flavored sprays are super ways to add a touch of taste, either before or after cooking foods, without adding lots of fat and calories.

Serving Sizes

I like to serve generous-sized pizza slices myself, so I generally figure that way when I list the number of slices per pizza. Yes, appetites do vary, and you know your gang better than I do, so, as always, you be the judge of how much to make. I do suggest cutting the dessert pizzas into smaller portions, though, since they're so filling.

Packaged Foods

Packaged food sizes may vary by brand. Generally, the sizes indicated in these recipes are average sizes. If you can't find the exact package size listed in the ingredients, whatever package is closest in size will usually do the trick.

The Building Blocks
Doughs and Sauces

The last time my grandchildren came over I was watching them play with building blocks, and their structures kept tumbling down. After many tries, they finally caught on that they had to have a solid base before it would work. You're probably wondering what this has to do with pizza. Well, if you think about it, there really is a similarity. No, I'm not talking about putting blocks on your pizza! I'm talking about the solid foundation you need before you can make a really great pizza: a super dough and a tasty sauce. Together they are the strength that makes an okay pizza into an awesome pizza. So, even if you haven't ever made pizza dough or sauce from scratch, flip through the following recipes and select the right dough and sauce for turning out your very own **"OOH IT'S SO GOOD!!™"**

The Building Blocks
Doughs and Sauces

HOMEMADE DOUGHS

Traditional Pizza Dough

1 pound dough

Here's how to make your homemade pizzas with authentic Italian-style crust. And with the help of your food processor, it's easy, easy, easy!

2¼ cups all-purpose flour, plus more if needed
1 package (¼ ounce) active dry yeast
1 teaspoon salt
1 cup very warm water (about 120°F.)
1 teaspoon sugar
1 tablespoon olive oil, divided

1. In a food processor that has been fitted with its steel cutting blade, place 2¼ cups flour, the yeast, and salt. Process for 3 to 5 seconds, until the ingredients are well mixed. In a small bowl, combine the water, sugar, and 2 teaspoons of the oil. With the processor running, slowly pour the water mixture through the feeding tube. After it is completely mixed, if the dough is too soft, add more flour 1 tablespoon at a time until a smooth ball forms. Process for 20 to 25 seconds to knead the dough.
2. Place the dough in a bowl that has been coated with nonstick vegetable spray; turn the dough. Cover with plastic wrap and allow to rise at room temperature for 35 to 40 minutes, until doubled in size.
3. Punch the dough down (see page xx), cover, and let sit for 10 minutes.
4. Using your fingertips or the heel of your hand, spread the dough to cover the bottom of a 12- to 14-inch pizza pan that has been

coated with nonstick vegetable spray. Push the dough up to the edge of the pan, forming a rim. If the dough is too sticky, dust it and your hands lightly with flour.

SPREADING DOUGH

Ahh!
A
MASSAGE!

5. With a fork, prick the dough 15 to 20 times.
6. Brush with the remaining 1 teaspoon oil.

NOTE: No food processor? No problem. Just place the 2¼ cups flour, yeast, and salt in a large bowl and mix until well blended. Slowly add the water mixture to the flour mixture until a crumbly dough forms. Turn onto a lightly floured surface and knead for 4 to 5 minutes, or until the dough is satiny smooth and has an elastic feel (see page xix). Add more flour 1 tablespoon at a time if necessary to achieve this consistency. Form into a ball and follow the directions from step 2 above.

Pizza Dough Variations

To create tasty dough variations, just follow the directions for Traditional Pizza Dough (page 3) and add these extra ingredients as suggested:

Caraway Seed Dough: Add 2 teaspoons caraway seeds while kneading the dough.

Cheese Dough: Add ¾ cup (3 ounces) shredded mozzarella cheese while kneading the dough.

Cornmeal Dough: Replace 1 cup of the flour with 1 cup cornmeal.

Cracked Black Pepper Dough: Add 2 teaspoons cracked black pepper to the flour and salt mixture. Oh, to crack or grind fresh black peppercorns, use a pepper mill or place them in a plastic bag and gently crush with a mallet.

Crushed Red Pepper Dough: Add 1½ teaspoons crushed red pepper to the flour and salt mixture.

Garlic Dough: Add 2 tablespoons minced garlic (6 garlic cloves) to the flour and salt mixture.

Herb Dough: Add 1 teaspoon dried basil and 1 teaspoon dried oregano to the flour and salt mixture.

Poppy Seed Dough: Add 1 tablespoon poppy seeds while kneading the dough.

Sesame Seed Dough: Add 1 tablespoon sesame seeds while kneading the dough. For added flavor, toast the sesame seeds first for 2 to 3 minutes in a 350°F. oven.

Sweet Dough: Add ¼ cup sugar to the flour and yeast, and reduce the salt to ½ teaspoon and the olive oil to 1 teaspoon. Also, in step 6, brush the top of the dough with 1 tablespoon melted butter instead of olive oil.

Whole Wheat Dough: Replace 1 cup of the flour with 1 cup whole wheat flour.

Deep-Dish Pizza Dough

1 pound dough

If you're looking for a pizza dough that will hold up to those heartier toppings, then this is your dough. You won't believe how easy it is to make...really!

3 cups all-purpose flour, plus more if needed

1 teaspoon salt

2 teaspoons sugar

1 package (¼ ounce) active dry yeast

1 cup very warm water (about 120°F.)

2 tablespoons olive oil, divided

1. In a large bowl, combine the flour and salt; set aside. In a small bowl, dissolve the sugar and yeast in the water. Add 1 tablespoon of the oil to the water mixture, then add to the flour. Mix with your hands until a soft ball forms.
2. Knead on a lightly floured surface for 5 to 7 minutes, until the dough is smooth and elastic (see page xix). If the dough is too sticky, add more flour 1 tablespoon at a time.
3. Place the dough in a bowl that has been coated with nonstick vegetable spray; turn the dough. Cover with plastic wrap and allow to rise at room temperature for 45 to 50 minutes, until doubled in size.
4. Punch the dough down (see page xx).
5. Coat a 12-inch deep-dish pizza pan or a 12-inch round cake pan with nonstick vegetable spray. Using your fingertips or the heel of your hand, spread the dough so that it covers the bottom of the pan and dough comes three quarters of the way up the sides.
6. Cover with plastic wrap and let sit for 10 minutes.
7. Uncover and brush with the remaining 1 tablespoon oil.

Quick Pizza Dough

1 pound dough

Sometimes we don't have time to wait for dough to rise. So here's the perfect solution for those times when we still want to make it ourselves, but with ready-made quickness!

2 cups all-purpose flour
2 teaspoons baking powder
$1/2$ teaspoon salt
$1/4$ teaspoon white pepper
$1/4$ cup ($1/2$ stick) butter, softened
$3/4$ cup milk
1 teaspoon vegetable oil

1. In a large bowl, combine the flour, baking powder, salt, and pepper. Add the butter and mix with your fingers until the mixture becomes crumbly. Stir in the milk and mix to form a dough.
2. Place on a lightly floured surface and knead for 5 to 6 minutes (see page xix).
3. With a floured rolling pin, roll the dough out to a 12- to 14-inch circle. Place on a 12- to 14-inch pizza pan that has been coated with nonstick vegetable spray.
4. Brush with the oil.

Cheesy Crust Dough

1 pound dough

Now you can keep up with the pizzerias that are offering cheese baked right in the crust of the pizza.

2¼ cups all-purpose flour, plus more if needed
1 package (¼ ounce) active dry yeast
1 teaspoon salt
1 cup very warm water (about 120°F.)
1 teaspoon sugar
1 tablespoon olive oil, divided
1 package (8 ounces) mozzarella string cheese (8 cheese sticks)

1. In a food processor that has been fitted with its steel cutting blade, place 2¼ cups flour, the yeast, and salt. Process for 3 to 5 seconds, until the ingredients are well mixed. In a small bowl, combine the water, sugar, and 2 teaspoons of the oil. With the processor running, slowly pour the water mixture through the feeding tube. After it is completely mixed, if the dough is too soft, add more flour 1 tablespoon at a time until a smooth ball forms. Process on "pulse" for 20 to 25 seconds to knead the dough.
2. Place the dough in a bowl that has been coated with nonstick vegetable spray; turn the dough. Cover with plastic wrap and allow to rise at room temperature for 35 to 40 minutes, until doubled in size.
3. Punch the dough down (see page xx), cover, and let sit for 10 minutes.
4. Using your fingertips or the heel of your hand, spread the dough to cover the bottom of a 12- to 14-inch pizza pan that has been coated with nonstick vegetable spray. Push the dough up to the edge of the pan, forming a rim. If the dough is too sticky, dust it and your hands lightly with flour.

5. With a fork, prick the dough 15 to 20 times.

6. Place the string cheese around the edge of the dough about 1 inch in from the edge and fold the dough over the cheese. Pinch the dough together with your fingers to seal. Brush with the remaining 1 teaspoon oil.

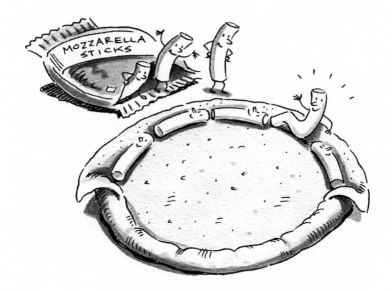

STORE-BOUGHT PIZZA DOUGHS

Ready-Made Pizza Dough

When you want to make homemade pizza but don't want to start from scratch with the dough, ready-made dough is the answer! Because it makes pizza-making so easy, ready-made dough is widely available now. It's usually stocked in the freezer section, but many supermarkets make fresh pizza dough daily, and it can be found in the baking or deli section of the market. You can often buy raw dough from local pizzerias, too. (Just call ahead to be sure they've got 1-pound packages of pizza dough ready for sale.) Here's how to prepare ready-made dough for topping:

1 pound store-bought pizza dough
1 teaspoon olive oil

1. If the dough is frozen, thaw at room temperature in a plastic bag for 3 to 4 hours. Keep out of direct sunlight.
2. Using your fingertips or the heel of your hand, spread the dough to cover the bottom of a 12- to 14-inch pizza pan that has been coated with nonstick vegetable spray. Push the dough up to the edge of the pan, forming a rim. If the dough is too sticky, dust it and your hands lightly with flour.
3. With a fork, prick the dough 15 to 20 times.
4. Brush with the oil.

Frozen Bread Dough

Frozen bread dough is a super option for your pizza, calzone, and focaccia bases. It comes in white, whole wheat, rye, and other varieties, so have a ball mixing and matching!

1 pound frozen bread dough
1 teaspoon olive oil

1. Thaw the bread dough according to the package directions.
2. Using your fingertips or the heel of your hand, spread the dough to cover the bottom of a 12- to 14-inch pizza pan that has been coated with nonstick vegetable spray. Push the dough up to the edge of the pan, forming a rim. If the dough is too sticky, dust it and your hands lightly with flour.
3. With a fork, prick the dough 15 to 20 times.
4. Brush with the oil.

Refrigerated All-Ready Pizza "Crust"*

This product is like pre-made dough in a tube. Usually found in the refrigerated area of the supermarket, with the refrigerated biscuits and rolls, it can be used as a base for pizzas and calzones, but it can't be used for deep-dish pizzas (there's not enough dough!). And since it's usually sold in 10- to 11-ounce packages (not a full pound of dough), these crusts tend to be a bit thinner, which means a few minutes less cooking time (but remember that each pizza's cooking time varies anyway, depending upon its toppings). So when using this type of dough, be especially aware of suggested recipe notes, such as "bake until the crust is crisp and brown."

1 package (10 to 11 ounces) refrigerated pizza dough
1 teaspoon olive oil

1. Open tube and unroll the "crust."
2. Using your fingertips or the heel of your hand, spread the dough to cover the bottom of a 12- to 14-inch pizza pan that has been coated with nonstick vegetable spray. Push the dough up to the edge of the pan, forming a rim. If the dough is too sticky, dust it and your hands lightly with flour.
3. With a fork, prick the dough 15 to 20 times.
4. Brush with the oil.

*The packages generally label this product as a "crust," but it's really a dough, since it's not formed or prebaked.

PREPARED PIZZA SHELLS
AND ALTERNATIVES

Prepared Pizza Shells

Using prepared pizza shells is by far the easiest way to make pizza. They may not be homemade, but they're sure a tasty, quick option. These shells come frozen, refrigerated, or shelf-stable and in thick and thin varieties, to suit every pizza taste.

One 12- to 14-inch prepared pizza shell

If the shell is frozen, thaw according to package directions. Place on a pizza pan and top according to specific recipe directions.

NOTE: These are not recommended for most dessert pizzas and will not work for calzones or stuffed pizzas.

Prepared Pizza
Shell Alternatives

"What should I do with this nice fresh Italian bread?" If you just can't decide, why not make a pizza? Alternative types of crusts are perfect for experimenting—and, after all, isn't that what pizza-making should be about...making it just the way you like it? Why not try using the following pizza base alternatives instead of pizza dough or a prepared shell? Here's how to use them in my pizza recipes that list "Prepared Pizza Shell" as an option:

Bagels: Split 6 bagels in half and place cut side up on a cookie sheet.

English Muffins: Split 6 English muffins in half and place cut side up on a cookie sheet. Place under a preheated broiler for 2 to 3 minutes, or until lightly toasted.

French Bread: Slice one 1-pound loaf in half lengthwise and place it cut side up on a cookie sheet. Place under a preheated broiler for 2 to 3 minutes, or until lightly browned.

Italian Bread: Slice one 1-pound loaf in half lengthwise and place it cut side up on a cookie sheet. Place under a preheated broiler for 2 to 3 minutes, or until lightly browned.

Pita Bread: Place four 6-inch pita breads browned side down on a cookie sheet.

PIZZA SAUCES

Spicy Chunky Pizza Sauce

2½ cups

Why not whip up a batch or two of this spicy sauce and keep it covered in your refrigerator for up to a week for adding a bit of zing to your pizzas? You can use it in place of regular pizza or spaghetti sauce in any recipe in this book (except the sweet pizzas, of course!).

1 can (28 ounces) crushed tomatoes
2 tablespoons tomato paste
1 teaspoon garlic powder
1 teaspoon dried basil
1 teaspoon onion powder
1 teaspoon cayenne pepper

In a large saucepan, combine all of the ingredients. Cook over low heat for 25 to 30 minutes, or until the sauce is thickened and the flavors have blended. Use immediately or let cool, then store, tightly covered, in the refrigerator until ready to use.

NOTE: Remember, there are no rules—a bit more cayenne pepper will really wake up those taste buds. Or you might want to mellow the flavor by reducing the cayenne pepper to ½ teaspoon.

"No Time" Homemade Pizza Sauce

I call this my "No Time" sauce 'cause you can put it together in a minute or two...really! And the homemade taste will speak for itself. You can use it in place of regular pizza or spaghetti sauce in any recipe in this book (except the sweet pizzas, of course!).

1 cup (8 ounces) tomato sauce
1/2 teaspoon dried oregano
1/4 teaspoon dried basil
1/8 teaspoon garlic powder
1/8 teaspoon onion powder
1/4 teaspoon sugar
2 teaspoons tomato paste

In a medium-sized bowl, combine all the ingredients and mix until well blended. Spread the sauce evenly over a pizza dough or crust as directed in your favorite pizza recipe.

NOTE: I know you're wondering if you can really make a pizza sauce without cooking it. Yes, you can! The trick is in cooking it right on the pizza. Boy, is that ever a timesaver.

White Pizza Sauce

1¹/₂ cups

Sometimes you want a pizza sauce that's different—one that doesn't have a tomato base. This white sauce is a super partner for any of your favorite toppings.

1 package (8 ounces) cream cheese, softened
³/₄ cup (6 ounces) sour cream
2 tablespoons grated Parmesan cheese
¹/₄ teaspoon white pepper

In a medium-sized bowl, combine all the ingredients; beat with an electric beater for about 3 minutes, until creamy and smooth. Top an unbaked pizza dough or a prepared pizza shell with this sauce and your favorite toppings.

NOTE: Bake an unbaked-dough pizza for 10 to 14 minutes and a prepared-pizza-shell pizza for 8 to 10 minutes, or until the crust is crisp and brown.

Homemade Pesto Sauce

About 1 1/2 cups

They've been enjoying pesto sauce for years in Italy, and lately it's become really popular here in America. Here's a homemade version that tastes like it's right from an Italian kitchen.

2 cups lightly packed fresh basil leaves
1 cup olive oil
1 cup grated Parmesan cheese
2 garlic cloves, crushed
1 teaspoon salt
1/2 cup pine nuts or walnuts, finely chopped

Combine all the ingredients in a blender or food processor and blend until smooth. Store in the refrigerator, covered, until ready to use.

Roasted Garlic

Most people think that garlic is always pungent, but when it's baked, it becomes really mellow. And made this way, it's soft enough to squeeze out and spread on anything from pizza dough and prepared pizza shells to Italian and other types of breads.

1 large bulb of fresh garlic
About 1 teaspoon olive oil
About ⅛ teaspoon coarse (kosher) salt

Preheat the oven to 325°F. Cut the garlic bulb in half crosswise and place cut sides up on a piece of aluminum foil. Lightly sprinkle the cut sides with oil and salt. Put the 2 halves back together and wrap tightly in the foil. Bake for 1½ to 2 hours, then open the warm bulb and use the soft garlic pulp as a spread in place of butter.

NOTE: Why not bake a few extras and refrigerate them (wrapped in the foil) for reheating? Just remove the foil and reheat in the microwave. Use within a few days.

Traditional Pizzas

Let's get started! And there's no better way than with traditional favorites. These are pizzas that have been around for generations. Now, that *doesn't* mean that they're boring! Uh-uh! When I talk about traditional pizzas, I mean the long-time winners like Garlic Pizza (page 38)—studded with minced garlic and smothered with two types of cheese, Chicago Deep-Dish Sausage Pizza (page 39)—full of ever-popular hot Italian sausage, and Pizza with "The Works" (page 28)—overflowing with all of the most universally favored toppings. You'll find most of these on menus everywhere from corner pizzerias to upscale wood-burning–oven pizza restaurants. And now they can be on *your* menu, too. So go ahead, bring a little pizza tradition into your kitchen—and don't be afraid to add a dash or two of pizzazz to make them your own.

Traditional Pizzas

No-Rules Cheese Pizza

6 to 8 slices

I should call this the **Mr. Food®** pizza. Why? Because when you make it, you've got limitless options! You can add any of the toppings on the next page (or any other favorites). Mix 'em, match 'em, and, remember, there are no rules!

Pizza base of your choice:

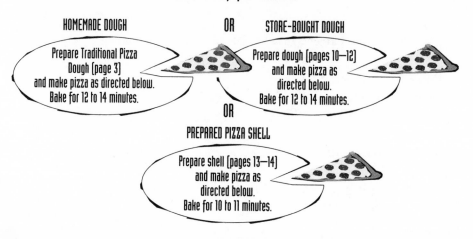

HOMEMADE DOUGH

Prepare Traditional Pizza Dough [page 3] and make pizza as directed below. Bake for 12 to 14 minutes.

OR

STORE-BOUGHT DOUGH

Prepare dough [pages 10–12] and make pizza as directed below. Bake for 12 to 14 minutes.

OR

PREPARED PIZZA SHELL

Prepare shell [pages 13–14] and make pizza as directed below. Bake for 10 to 11 minutes.

¾ cup pizza or spaghetti sauce
¼ cup grated Parmesan cheese
1½ cups (6 ounces) shredded
  mozzarella cheese

½ teaspoon dried basil
½ teaspoon dried oregano

Preheat the oven to 450°F. Spread the sauce evenly over the prepared base. Top with the Parmesan cheese, then the mozzarella cheese. Sprinkle with the basil and oregano (and other favorite toppings, if desired—see page 25) and bake as directed above, or until the crust is crisp and brown. Cut and serve.

Toppings for Cheese Pizza

If you're gonna turn your kitchen into a pizzeria, then you need to know how much of any topping you'll need to put on a pizza. This list will take all of the guesswork out of making pizza. These amounts are a guide for when you're using just one topping on a whole 12- to 14-inch pizza. If you want to mix and match, cut down the amount of each topping. For example, if you use two toppings, cut each one in half or, if you use four toppings, use a quarter of the amount given for each, right? You've got it!

Extra Cheese: 1 extra cup (4 ounces) shredded cheese

Pepperoni: 2 to 3 ounces, thinly sliced (about 35 slices)

Sausage: 8 ounces Italian sausage, cooked and crumbled

Fresh Bell Pepper: 1 medium-sized bell pepper, cut into 1/4-inch strips

Roasted Peppers: 1 jar (7.5 ounces) roasted peppers, drained, patted dry, and cut into chunks or 1/4-inch strips

Fresh Mushrooms: 5 ounces, sliced (about 2 cups)

Canned Mushrooms: 1 can (7 ounces) sliced mushrooms or mushroom stems and pieces

Onion: 1 large onion, thinly sliced and lightly sautéed

Fresh Spinach: 5 ounces cleaned fresh spinach (1/2 a 10-ounce bag)

Chopped Frozen Spinach: 1 package (10 ounces), thawed and well drained

Broccoli: 3 cups steamed fresh broccoli florets (If using frozen, just thaw and drain.)

Black Olives: 1 can (2.25 ounces) sliced black olives, drained (about 1/2 cup)

Salami: 3 ounces, thinly sliced

Anchovies: 2 cans (about 2 ounces each), drained

Pizza Margherita

6 to 8 slices

I first had this type of pizza in a small pizza parlor in the Northeast, and after just one bite, I knew I had to make a quick version just like it to share with you!

Pizza base of your choice:

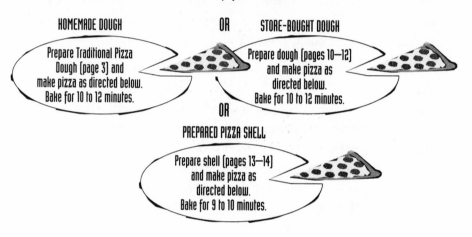

HOMEMADE DOUGH OR **STORE-BOUGHT DOUGH**

Prepare Traditional Pizza Dough (page 3) and make pizza as directed below. Bake for 10 to 12 minutes.

Prepare dough (pages 10–12) and make pizza as directed below. Bake for 10 to 12 minutes.

OR

PREPARED PIZZA SHELL

Prepare shell (pages 13–14) and make pizza as directed below. Bake for 9 to 10 minutes.

1 can (14½ ounces) whole tomatoes, drained and coarsely chopped
1 tablespoon chopped fresh basil
½ teaspoon dried oregano

½ teaspoon garlic powder
½ teaspoon salt
¼ teaspoon black pepper
4 ounces fresh mozzarella cheese (like Buffalo), patted dry and sliced ⅛ inch thick

Preheat the oven to 450°F. In a small bowl, combine all of the topping ingredients except the mozzarella cheese; mix well. Spread the mixture evenly over the prepared base, then top with the mozzarella slices. Bake as directed above, or until the crust is crisp and brown. Cut and serve.

Nutty Pesto Pizza

6 to 8 slices

Pesto is sure becoming more and more popular today, and whether it's store-bought or homemade, it's a winning pizza topping.

Pizza base of your choice:

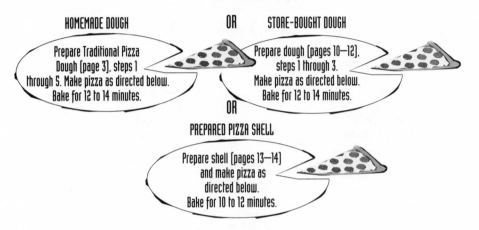

HOMEMADE DOUGH

Prepare Traditional Pizza Dough (page 3), steps 1 through 5. Make pizza as directed below. Bake for 12 to 14 minutes.

OR

STORE-BOUGHT DOUGH

Prepare dough (pages 10–12), steps 1 through 3. Make pizza as directed below. Bake for 12 to 14 minutes.

OR

PREPARED PIZZA SHELL

Prepare shell (pages 13–14) and make pizza as directed below. Bake for 10 to 12 minutes.

1/3 cup Homemade Pesto Sauce (page 18) or prepared pesto
1/2 cup (2 ounces) shredded mozzarella cheese
1/2 cup grated Parmesan cheese
1/2 cup coarsely chopped walnuts

Preheat the oven to 450°F. Spread the pesto sauce evenly over the prepared base. Sprinkle with the cheeses and top with the chopped walnuts. Bake as directed above, or until the crust is crisp and brown. Cut and serve.

NOTE: Be especially careful when removing the pizza from the oven, because the oil on the top of the pizza will be very hot.

Pizza with "The Works"

6 to 8 slices

In Troy, New York, where I grew up, there was a pizza parlor that made a special pizza piled with loads of my favorite toppings. It had *everything* on it, so they called it "The Works." Now I'm sharing my shortcut version. (Bet you'll love it, too!)

Pizza base of your choice:

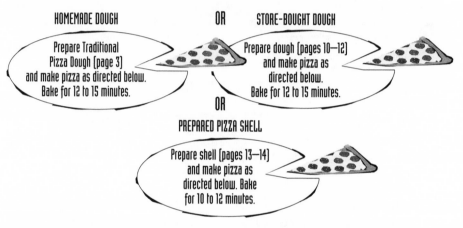

HOMEMADE DOUGH — Prepare Traditional Pizza Dough (page 3) and make pizza as directed below. Bake for 12 to 15 minutes.

OR

STORE-BOUGHT DOUGH — Prepare dough (pages 10–12) and make pizza as directed below. Bake for 12 to 15 minutes.

OR

PREPARED PIZZA SHELL — Prepare shell (pages 13–14) and make pizza as directed below. Bake for 10 to 12 minutes.

½ cup pizza or spaghetti sauce
8 ounces hot or sweet bulk Italian sausage, cooked and crumbled
1½ ounces pepperoni, thinly sliced (about 25 slices)
½ cup chopped red bell pepper
1 small onion, chopped (about ½ cup)

1 can (7 ounces) mushroom stems and pieces, drained
1 can (2.25 ounces) sliced black olives, drained (about ½ cup)
1 can (1.8 ounces) anchovy fillets, drained
1 cup (4 ounces) shredded mozzarella cheese

Preheat the oven to 450°F. Spread the sauce evenly over the prepared base. Top with the remaining ingredients in the order listed, ending with the mozzarella cheese. Bake as directed above, or until the crust is crisp and brown. Cut and serve.

NOTE: Add more or less of any of the toppings to make it your own special work of "Art."

White Pizza

6 to 8 slices

I'm dreaming of a white pizza.... Okay, I know the song says something else, but this pizza tastes and smells as special as any holiday!

Pizza base of your choice:

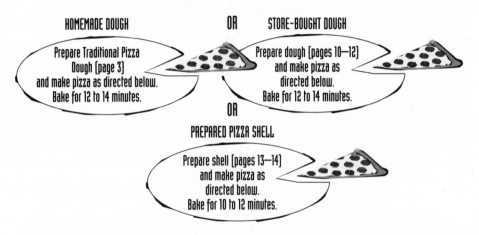

HOMEMADE DOUGH

Prepare Traditional Pizza Dough (page 3) and make pizza as directed below. Bake for 12 to 14 minutes.

OR

STORE-BOUGHT DOUGH

Prepare dough (pages 10–12) and make pizza as directed below. Bake for 12 to 14 minutes.

OR

PREPARED PIZZA SHELL

Prepare shell (pages 13–14) and make pizza as directed below. Bake for 10 to 12 minutes.

1 cup (about 9 ounces) ricotta cheese
1 tablespoon chopped garlic (3 cloves)
1 cup (4 ounces) shredded mozzarella cheese, divided

$1/3$ cup grated Parmesan cheese
$1/2$ teaspoon Italian seasoning
$1/4$ teaspoon onion powder
$1/4$ teaspoon salt
$1/8$ teaspoon white pepper

Preheat the oven to 450°F. If using Traditional Pizza Dough or store-bought dough, bake for 7 to 9 minutes, just until golden. Remove from the oven and set aside. Meanwhile, in a medium-sized bowl, combine all the topping ingredients except $3/4$ cup of the mozzarella cheese; mix well. Spread the mixture over the prepared crust and top with the remaining mozzarella cheese. Bake as directed above, or until the crust is crisp and brown. Cut and serve.

NOTE: A sprinkle of chopped fresh parsley on the top sure adds a burst of color to this!

Four Seasons Pizza

6 to 8 slices

Don't let the name confuse you. It's really very simple—the four seasons come from the different toppings on each quarter of the pizza. And I hope you'll eat this one in *every* season of the year!

Pizza base of your choice:

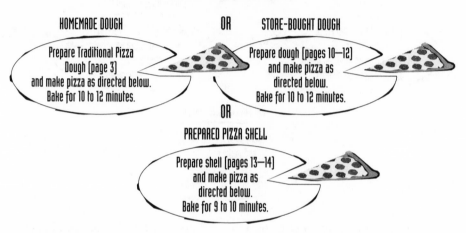

HOMEMADE DOUGH   **OR**   **STORE-BOUGHT DOUGH**

Prepare Traditional Pizza Dough [page 3] and make pizza as directed below. Bake for 10 to 12 minutes.

Prepare dough [pages 10–12] and make pizza as directed below. Bake for 10 to 12 minutes.

OR

PREPARED PIZZA SHELL

Prepare shell [pages 13–14] and make pizza as directed below. Bake for 9 to 10 minutes.

3/4 cup pizza or spaghetti sauce
1 cup (4 ounces) shredded mozzarella cheese
1 teaspoon dried oregano
2 plum tomatoes, sliced crosswise, 1/4 inch thick
1/4 cup coarsely chopped fresh basil
3 artichoke hearts (1/2 a 14-ounce can), drained and coarsely chopped

1 can (4 ounces) pimientos, drained and chopped
1 ounce prosciutto or thinly sliced deli ham, cut into 1/2-inch strips

Preheat the oven to 450°F. Spread the sauce evenly over the prepared base and top with the mozzarella cheese. Sprinkle with the oregano. Use a knife to mark the dough into 4 equal sections. Place the tomatoes on 1 section, overlapping them, and top with the basil. Top another section with the artichokes. Top the third section with the pimientos, and lay out the prosciutto on the fourth section. Bake as directed above, or until the crust is crisp and brown. Cut and serve.

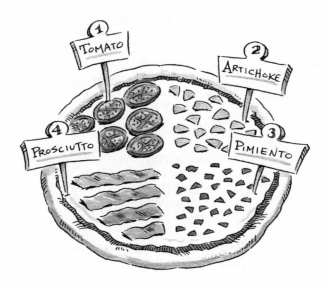

Veggie-Drawer Pizza

6 to 8 slices

If you're like me, your vegetable drawer has a little of this and a little of that in it. Well, here's the perfect way to use up all those "aging" veggies—and you'll love them all over again!

Pizza base of your choice:

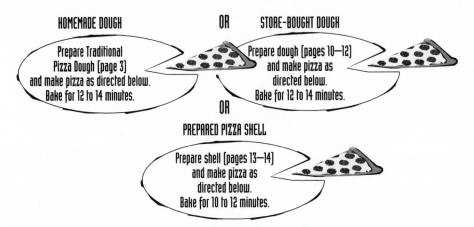

HOMEMADE DOUGH OR **STORE-BOUGHT DOUGH**

Prepare Traditional Pizza Dough (page 3) and make pizza as directed below. Bake for 12 to 14 minutes.

Prepare dough (pages 10–12) and make pizza as directed below. Bake for 12 to 14 minutes.

OR

PREPARED PIZZA SHELL

Prepare shell (pages 13–14) and make pizza as directed below. Bake for 10 to 12 minutes.

2 tablespoons vegetable oil
3/4 cup sliced fresh mushrooms
1/2 cup broccoli florets
1/2 a medium-sized green bell pepper, sliced
1 small onion, chopped (about 1/2 cup)
1/2 teaspoon garlic powder
1/4 teaspoon dried oregano

1 cup pizza or spaghetti sauce
1 can (2.25 ounces) sliced black olives, drained (about 1/2 cup)
1 small tomato, coarsely chopped (about 3/4 cup)
1 cup (4 ounces) shredded mozzarella cheese
1/4 cup grated Parmesan cheese

Preheat the oven to 450°F. In a medium-sized skillet, heat the oil over medium heat. Add the mushrooms, broccoli, bell pepper, onion, garlic powder, and oregano and sauté for 4 to 5 minutes, or just until the broccoli turns bright green; remove from the heat and drain the excess liquid. Spread the sauce evenly over the prepared base and top with the vegetable mixture. Sprinkle with the olives and tomato, then top with the cheeses. Bake as directed above, or until the crust is crisp and brown. Cut and serve.

Tri-Color Roasted Pepper Pizza

6 to 8 slices

Wow! This pizza is so colorful that you might have to put your sunglasses on before you eat it!

Pizza base of your choice:

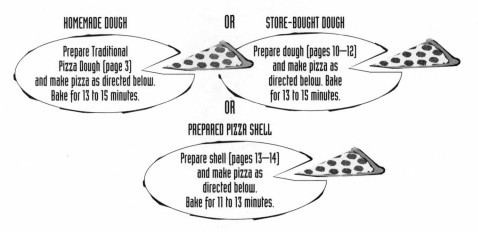

HOMEMADE DOUGH

Prepare Traditional Pizza Dough (page 3) and make pizza as directed below. Bake for 13 to 15 minutes.

OR

STORE-BOUGHT DOUGH

Prepare dough (pages 10–12) and make pizza as directed below. Bake for 13 to 15 minutes.

OR

PREPARED PIZZA SHELL

Prepare shell (pages 13–14) and make pizza as directed below. Bake for 11 to 13 minutes.

2 tablespoons olive oil
1/4 teaspoon garlic powder
1/4 teaspoon onion powder
1/4 teaspoon salt
1/4 teaspoon black pepper

3 medium-sized bell peppers (red, green, and yellow, or any combination), sliced into 1-inch strips
2/3 cup pizza or spaghetti sauce
1 package (6 ounces) sliced mozzarella cheese

Preheat the oven to 450°F. In a small bowl, combine the oil, garlic powder, onion powder, salt, and black pepper. Add the bell peppers and toss to coat, then place in a 9"× 13" baking dish. Bake for 20 to 25 minutes, or until the peppers are fork-tender. Spread the sauce over the prepared base and cover with the mozzarella slices. Place the roasted peppers over the cheese and bake as directed above, or until the crust is crisp and brown. Cut and serve.

NOTE: Sure, you can make this with three bell peppers that are all the same color, but you won't get the really colorful effect. So, try it with three different colors—it'll be worth the effort. This recipe is especially good when it's made with Spicy Chunky Pizza Sauce (page 15).

Broccoli Ricotta Pizza

6 to 8 slices

There's a popular recipe for a broccoli and ricotta cheese casserole that always gets rave reviews. Now it's time to put the same idea to work on a pizza. That is, only if you're ready for more raves!

Pizza base of your choice:

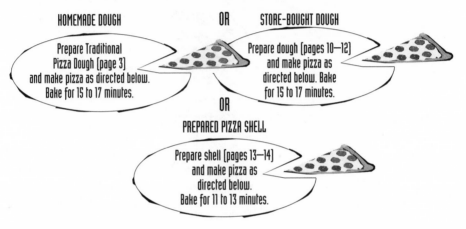

HOMEMADE DOUGH

Prepare Traditional Pizza Dough (page 3) and make pizza as directed below. Bake for 15 to 17 minutes.

OR

STORE-BOUGHT DOUGH

Prepare dough (pages 10–12) and make pizza as directed below. Bake for 15 to 17 minutes.

OR

PREPARED PIZZA SHELL

Prepare shell (pages 13–14) and make pizza as directed below. Bake for 11 to 13 minutes.

1 cup (about 8 ounces) ricotta cheese
1/2 teaspoon garlic powder
1/2 teaspoon dried basil
3/4 teaspoon seasoned salt
1/8 teaspoon black pepper

1 package (10 ounces) frozen chopped broccoli, thawed and well drained
1 cup (4 ounces) shredded mozzarella cheese

Preheat the oven to 450°F. If using Traditional Pizza Dough or store-bought dough, bake for 7 to 9 minutes, just until golden. Remove from the oven and set aside. Meanwhile, in a medium-sized bowl, combine the ricotta cheese, garlic powder, basil, seasoned salt, and pepper; mix well. Spread the mixture over the prepared crust, then layer the broccoli evenly over the top. Sprinkle with the mozzarella cheese and bake as directed above, or until the crust is crisp and brown. Cut and serve.

NOTE: Sure, use low-fat cheeses to keep the fat and calories down.

Meatball Pizza

6 to 8 slices

I used to think that meatballs belonged only on top of spaghetti, but I've changed my mind! How 'bout you?

Pizza base of your choice:

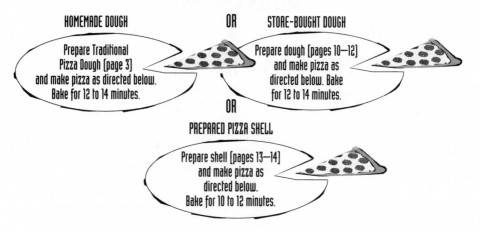

HOMEMADE DOUGH

Prepare Traditional Pizza Dough (page 3) and make pizza as directed below. Bake for 12 to 14 minutes.

OR

STORE-BOUGHT DOUGH

Prepare dough (pages 10–12) and make pizza as directed below. Bake for 12 to 14 minutes.

OR

PREPARED PIZZA SHELL

Prepare shell (pages 13–14) and make pizza as directed below. Bake for 10 to 12 minutes.

12 ounces ready-made frozen meatballs (1-inch size), thawed and cut in half
1 cup pizza or spaghetti sauce

1 cup (4 ounces) shredded mozzarella cheese
1/2 teaspoon Italian seasoning

Preheat the oven to 450°F. In a medium-sized bowl, toss the meatballs with the sauce. Spread the mixture evenly over the prepared base with the meatballs flat side down. Top with the cheese and sprinkle with the Italian seasoning. Bake as directed above, or until the crust is crisp and brown. Cut and serve.

NOTE: I wanted to make this as simple as possible, but of course you can use your favorite homemade meatballs. It'll sure taste great either way! And if you'd like to make homemade sauce, try "No Time" Homemade Pizza Sauce (page 16).

Garlic Pizza

6 to 8 slices

If you want to taste "classic" Italian pizza, then this one's for you. Ooh, that garlic, Parmesan, and mozzarella! (And you thought pizza needed tomato sauce!)

Pizza base of your choice:

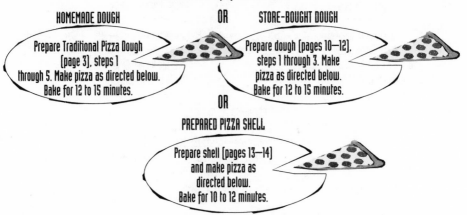

HOMEMADE DOUGH OR **STORE-BOUGHT DOUGH**

Prepare Traditional Pizza Dough [page 3], steps 1 through 5. Make pizza as directed below. Bake for 12 to 15 minutes.

Prepare dough [pages 10–12], steps 1 through 3. Make pizza as directed below. Bake for 12 to 15 minutes.

OR

PREPARED PIZZA SHELL

Prepare shell [pages 13–14] and make pizza as directed below. Bake for 10 to 12 minutes.

2 tablespoons butter, melted
2 tablespoons chopped garlic
 (5 to 6 cloves)
1/2 teaspoon salt
1/4 cup grated Parmesan cheese

1 cup (4 ounces) shredded
 mozzarella cheese
1 tablespoon chopped fresh
 parsley

Preheat the oven to 450°F. In a small bowl, combine the butter, garlic, and salt; mix well. Brush the mixture evenly over the prepared base, then top with the cheeses and parsley. Bake as directed above, or until the crust is crisp and brown. Cut and serve.

Chicago Deep-Dish Sausage Pizza

6 to 8 slices

Do you think there's a relationship between Chicago's deep-dish pizzas and its nickname as the Windy City? Let me know your answer after this pizza blows you away!

Pizza dough of your choice:

HOMEMADE DOUGH   **OR**   **STORE-BOUGHT DOUGH**

Prepare Deep-Dish Pizza Dough [page 6] and make pizza as directed below. Bake for 20 to 25 minutes.

Prepare dough [pages 10–11] and make pizza as directed below. Bake for 20 to 25 minutes.

8 ounces hot Italian sausage, casings removed
1 medium-sized green bell pepper, cut into ¼-inch strips
5 ounces fresh mushrooms, sliced (about 2 cups)

1 teaspoon dried basil
¾ cup pizza or spaghetti sauce
1 cup (4 ounces) shredded mozzarella cheese
¼ cup grated Parmesan cheese

Preheat the oven to 450°F. In a large skillet, cook and stir the sausage over medium-low heat until no pink remains. Stir in the pepper, mushrooms, and basil; reduce the heat to low. Cook for 5 to 6 minutes, until the vegetables are just tender, then drain off the excess liquid. Spread the sauce evenly over the prepared base and top with the sausage mixture, then the mozzarella and Parmesan cheeses. Bake as directed above, or until the crust is crisp and brown. Cut and serve.

NOTE: You can make a milder version of this by using mild sausage. Use a sausage that's got the degree of spiciness your gang enjoys.

Pizzas from Around the World

Curry Shrimp Pizza...?! Taco Pizza...?! "Oui" Brie Pizza...?! Yes, yes, yes! Once you flipped to this page, you had to know right away that you were past the traditional pizzas. These combinations are everything *but* traditional!

I have to admit that I enjoy cross-cultural cooking. That's when you make a dish from one country and add a taste or style from another country. For example, with Peking Chicken Pizza (page 55), you get the blend of a crispy pizza shell with the taste of a Chinese favorite. Then there's Chicken Satay Pizza (page 60), made with peanut butter, soy sauce, and cayenne pepper, which is an exciting twist on a Thai favorite. Maybe we can't achieve world peace by joining these interesting tastes, but it sure is nice to think about as we take a trip around the world with every bite!

So now you know that no matter what type of food you're in the mood for, you can create it on a pizza shell...with a little help from me.

Pizzas from Around the World

Taco Pizza

6 to 8 slices

Whenever I eat crispy tacos, the shells break apart and the filling falls out. So now I make tacos pizza-style and get all the "ooh"s and "aah"s in every bite!

Pizza base of your choice:

HOMEMADE DOUGH   **OR**   **STORE-BOUGHT DOUGH**

Prepare Traditional Pizza Dough [page 3] and make pizza as directed below. Bake for 14 to 16 minutes.

Prepare dough [pages 10–12] and make pizza as directed below. Bake for 14 to 16 minutes.

OR

PREPARED PIZZA SHELL

Prepare shell [pages 13–14] and make pizza as directed below. Bake for 10 to 12 minutes.

½ pound ground beef
2 tablespoons taco seasoning mix (about ½ a 1.25-ounce package)
1 jar (16 ounces) salsa, well drained
1 cup (4 ounces) shredded Monterey Jack cheese
1 can (2.25 ounces) sliced black olives, drained (about ½ cup)

½ cup coarsely crushed tortilla chips
1 cup (4 ounces) shredded Cheddar cheese
1 cup shredded or thinly sliced iceberg lettuce
1 medium-sized tomato, coarsely chopped (about 1¼ cups)

Preheat the oven to 450°F. In a medium-sized skillet, brown the ground beef over medium-high heat for 5 to 7 minutes, or until no pink remains. Drain off the excess liquid, then reduce the heat to low. Add the taco seasoning and simmer for 2 minutes, stirring occasionally; remove from the heat. Spread the salsa over the prepared base. Top with the Monterey Jack, then the beef mixture, olives, tortilla chips, and Cheddar. Bake as directed above, or until the crust is crisp and brown. Top with the lettuce and tomato, then cut and serve.

NOTE: Flavored tortilla chips can add new taste to this recipe, so why not try ranch-flavored chips one time, spicy another, and on and on...the variations are almost endless!

Chicken Parmigiana Pizza

6 to 8 slices

Whenever we go out to an Italian restaurant with my son and daughter-in-law, one of them always orders chicken parmigiana, and the other orders cheese pizza. Well, I bet this will be a favorite in their house in no time!

Pizza base of your choice:

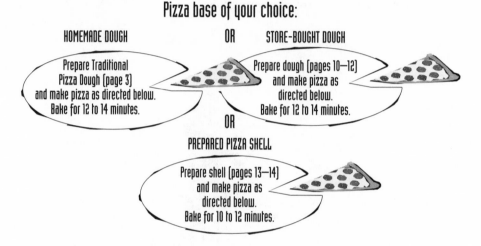

HOMEMADE DOUGH OR **STORE-BOUGHT DOUGH**

Prepare Traditional Pizza Dough [page 3] and make pizza as directed below. Bake for 12 to 14 minutes.

Prepare dough [pages 10–12] and make pizza as directed below. Bake for 12 to 14 minutes.

OR

PREPARED PIZZA SHELL

Prepare shell [pages 13–14] and make pizza as directed below. Bake for 10 to 12 minutes.

½ cup pizza or spaghetti sauce
1 cup (4 ounces) shredded
    mozzarella cheese
10 ready-made chicken nuggets,
    thawed if frozen, quartered

½ teaspoon dried basil
½ teaspoon dried oregano

Preheat the oven to 450°F. Spread the sauce evenly over the prepared base. Sprinkle with the cheese, then place the chicken pieces evenly over the cheese. Sprinkle with the basil and oregano and bake as directed above, or until the crust is crisp and brown. Cut and serve.

NOTE: Ready-made chicken nuggets are available in the supermarket freezer section.

Polynesian Pizza

6 to 8 slices

Did you know that the hula dance uses hand and body language to tell a story? Yup, and guess what? This pizza tells a story, too... mmm, a very satisfying story at that!

Pizza base of your choice:

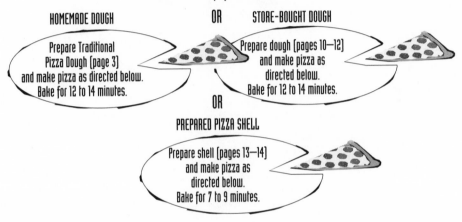

HOMEMADE DOUGH OR **STORE-BOUGHT DOUGH**

Prepare Traditional Pizza Dough (page 3) and make pizza as directed below. Bake for 12 to 14 minutes.

Prepare dough (pages 10–12) and make pizza as directed below. Bake for 12 to 14 minutes.

OR

PREPARED PIZZA SHELL

Prepare shell (pages 13–14) and make pizza as directed below. Bake for 7 to 9 minutes.

1 cup diced cooked ham (about ½ pound, cut into ½-inch cubes)
1 can (8 ounces) pineapple tidbits, drained and juice reserved

½ cup maraschino cherries, drained and sliced in half
¼ cup firmly packed light brown sugar
1 tablespoon cornstarch
1 tablespoon water

Preheat the oven to 450°F. In a medium-sized bowl, combine the ham, pineapple tidbits, and cherries; set aside. In a small saucepan, combine the reserved pineapple juice and the brown sugar and bring just to a boil over medium heat; reduce the heat to low. In a small bowl, dissolve the cornstarch in the water, then add to the juice mixture and stir until thickened. Add the ham mixture and stir until well coated. Spread evenly onto the prepared pizza base and bake as directed above, or until the crust is crisp and brown. Cut and serve.

NOTE: What a super way to use leftover ham after the holidays. And if you don't have pineapple tidbits, use pineapple chunks—just cut them in half.

Teriyaki Chicken Pizza

6 to 8 slices

Hmm...Should I have Japanese food or pizza? Here's a way to satisfy your craving for both! (And the Sesame Seed Dough really adds to the great flavor!)

Pizza base of your choice:

HOMEMADE DOUGH   OR   **STORE-BOUGHT DOUGH**

Prepare Sesame Seed Dough [page 5] and make pizza as directed below. Bake for 12 to 15 minutes.

Prepare dough [pages 10–12] and make pizza as directed below. Bake for 12 to 15 minutes.

OR

PREPARED PIZZA SHELL

Prepare shell [pages 13–14] and make pizza as directed below. Bake for 10 to 12 minutes.

1/4 cup soy sauce
1/4 cup firmly packed light brown sugar
1/2 teaspoon garlic powder
1/2 teaspoon ground ginger
1 medium-sized red bell pepper, cut into 1/4-inch strips

2 teaspoons cornstarch
1 teaspoon water
2 cups diced cooked chicken (about 1/2 pound)
1/2 cup sliced scallions (3 to 4 scallions)

Preheat the oven to 450°F. If using Sesame Seed Dough or store-bought dough, bake for 7 to 9 minutes, just until golden. Remove from the oven and set aside. Meanwhile, in a medium-sized skillet, combine the soy sauce, brown sugar, garlic powder, and ginger and bring to a boil over medium heat. Add the pepper strips and cook for 4 to 5 minutes, or until soft. In a small bowl, dissolve the cornstarch in the water, then add to the pepper mixture and stir until thickened. Remove from the heat and stir in the chicken until evenly coated. Spread the chicken mixture evenly over the crust and bake as directed above, or until the crust is crisp and brown. Remove from the oven and sprinkle with the scallions. Cut and serve.

Greek Pizza

6 to 8 slices

At first this sounded crazy to me, but then I thought, "Wait a minute! Isn't pizza just like a big pita with toppings?" Well, almost! And once you try your pizza with these Greek toppings, you'll be a believer, too!

Pizza base of your choice:

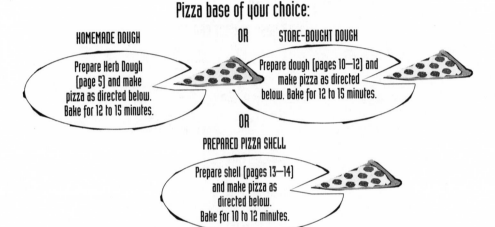

HOMEMADE DOUGH

Prepare Herb Dough [page 5] and make pizza as directed below. Bake for 12 to 15 minutes.

OR

STORE-BOUGHT DOUGH

Prepare dough [pages 10–12] and make pizza as directed below. Bake for 12 to 15 minutes.

OR

PREPARED PIZZA SHELL

Prepare shell [pages 13–14] and make pizza as directed below. Bake for 10 to 12 minutes.

1 cup pizza or spaghetti sauce
5 ounces fresh spinach (½ a 10-ounce bag), washed, dried, and chopped
1 large tomato, seeded and chopped (about 2 cups)
½ large cucumber, peeled, seeded, and cut into ½-inch cubes (about 1½ cups)

1 can (2.25 ounces) sliced black olives, drained (about ½ cup)
4 ounces feta cheese, crumbled (1 cup)
1 teaspoon salt
¾ cup (3 ounces) shredded mozzarella cheese

Preheat the oven to 450°F. If using Herb Dough or store-bought dough, bake for 7 to 9 minutes, just until golden. Remove from the oven and spread the sauce evenly over the crust. Top with the remaining ingredients in the order listed. Bake as directed above, or until the crust is crisp and brown. Cut and serve.

Chicken Fajita Pizza

6 to 8 slices

Fajitas are a great Tex-Mex meal, but everybody's got to work for it! Instead of doing all that layering and dolloping at the table, why not just make a fajita pizza? It's the perfect solution! (And if you're like me, you like a lot of cheese on your fajitas. That's why I use the cheese-stuffed dough with this one.)

Pizza base of your choice:

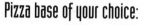

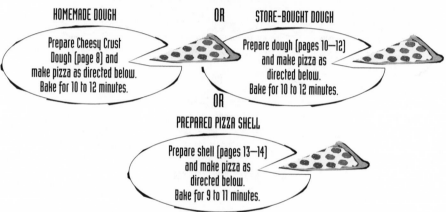

HOMEMADE DOUGH OR **STORE-BOUGHT DOUGH**

Prepare Cheesy Crust Dough (page 8) and make pizza as directed below. Bake for 10 to 12 minutes.

Prepare dough (pages 10–12) and make pizza as directed below. Bake for 10 to 12 minutes.

OR

PREPARED PIZZA SHELL

Prepare shell (pages 13–14) and make pizza as directed below. Bake for 9 to 11 minutes.

1 tablespoon vegetable oil
1 medium-sized onion, halved and sliced into ¼-inch strips
1 medium-sized green bell pepper, sliced into ¼-inch strips
4 boneless, skinless chicken breast halves (about 1 pound), cut into ¼-inch cubes

1 envelope (1.27 ounces) fajita seasoning
¼ cup water
1 cup (4 ounces) shredded Mexican cheese blend
1 cup (8 ounces) sour cream
1 medium-sized tomato, chopped (about 1¼ cups)

Preheat the oven to 450°F. In a large skillet, heat the oil over medium heat. Add the onion, pepper, and chicken cubes. Cook and stir for 10 minutes, or until the vegetables are tender and the chicken is no longer pink. Add the fajita seasoning and water, stirring until blended. Reduce the heat to low, cover, and simmer for 3 minutes. Spoon the chicken mixture onto the prepared base and top with the shredded cheese. Bake as directed above, or until the crust is crisp and brown. Just before serving, dollop the sour cream on the top and sprinkle with the tomato. Cut and serve.

NOTE: A few dollops (about 3/4 cup) of guacamole will add a super, authentic touch to this. Olé!

French Onion Soup Pizza

6 to 8 slices

Think back to the last time you had really good French onion soup...Mmm! It had lots of onions, a hint of red wine, and, of course, lots of bubbling melted cheese. Well, stop reminiscing and start making this recipe so you can have that great taste on your lips again in no time!

Pizza base of your choice:

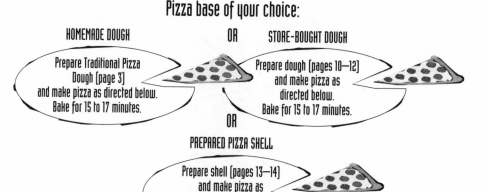

HOMEMADE DOUGH OR **STORE-BOUGHT DOUGH**

Prepare Traditional Pizza Dough (page 3) and make pizza as directed below. Bake for 15 to 17 minutes.

Prepare dough (pages 10–12) and make pizza as directed below. Bake for 15 to 17 minutes.

OR

PREPARED PIZZA SHELL

Prepare shell (pages 13–14) and make pizza as directed below. Bake for 10 to 12 minutes.

2 tablespoons olive oil
1 tablespoon chopped garlic
  (3 cloves)
4 medium-sized onions, sliced
  1/4 inch thick

3/4 teaspoon salt
3 tablespoons dry red wine
1 cup (4 ounces) shredded Swiss
  cheese
1/3 cup grated Parmesan cheese

Preheat the oven to 450°F. In a large skillet, heat the oil over medium-high heat. Add the garlic, onions, and salt and sauté for 10 to 12 minutes, or until the garlic and onions are well browned. Add the wine and cook for 1 to 2 more minutes. Spoon the onion mixture over the prepared base and top with the Swiss and Parmesan cheeses. Bake as directed above, or until the crust is crisp and brown. Cut and serve.

Peking Chicken Pizza

6 to 8 slices

Put away the chopsticks and get ready for an easy pizza version of Peking duck! And 'cause everybody thinks it's really complicated to make, you'd better keep it a secret...tell them no "Peking."

Pizza base of your choice:

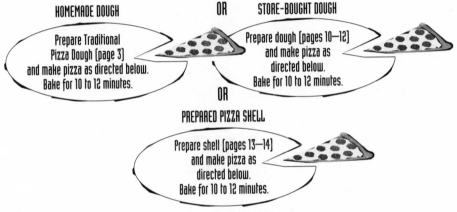

HOMEMADE DOUGH

Prepare Traditional Pizza Dough (page 3) and make pizza as directed below. Bake for 10 to 12 minutes.

OR

STORE-BOUGHT DOUGH

Prepare dough (pages 10–12) and make pizza as directed below. Bake for 10 to 12 minutes.

OR

PREPARED PIZZA SHELL

Prepare shell (pages 13–14) and make pizza as directed below. Bake for 10 to 12 minutes.

1 tablespoon vegetable oil
8 ounces boneless, skinless
   chicken thighs (2 to 3 thighs),
   cut into 1/8-inch strips

1/2 teaspoon salt
1/2 cup hoisin sauce
1/4 cup chopped scallions

Preheat the oven to 450°F. In a medium-sized skillet, heat the oil over medium heat. Sprinkle the chicken with the salt and sauté for 4 to 6 minutes, or until no pink remains. Drain off the excess liquid, then add the hoisin sauce to the skillet, stirring until the chicken is well coated. Spread the chicken evenly over the prepared base and bake as directed above, or until the crust is crisp and brown. Remove from the oven and sprinkle with the scallions. Cut and serve.

NOTE: Hoisin sauce can usually be found in the international section of the supermarket (or wherever they keep the soy sauce).

"Oui" Brie Pizza

6 to 8 slices

If you thought you could use only mozzarella cheese on pizza... No, no, no! French-style Brie adds lots of "Oui, oui, oui!" to this pizza!

Pizza base of your choice:

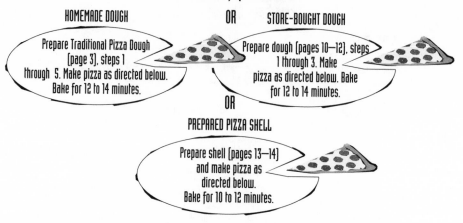

HOMEMADE DOUGH

Prepare Traditional Pizza Dough (page 3), steps 1 through 5. Make pizza as directed below. Bake for 12 to 14 minutes.

OR

STORE-BOUGHT DOUGH

Prepare dough (pages 10–12), steps 1 through 3. Make pizza as directed below. Bake for 12 to 14 minutes.

OR

PREPARED PIZZA SHELL

Prepare shell (pages 13–14) and make pizza as directed below. Bake for 10 to 12 minutes.

$1/3$ cup Homemade Pesto Sauce (page 18) or prepared pesto
1 small wheel ($4^1/2$ ounces) Brie cheese, cut into 16 wedges

2 cans ($4^1/2$ ounces each) pimientos, drained and chopped

Preheat the oven to 450°F. Spread the pesto sauce evenly over the prepared base. Place the Brie wedges evenly over the sauce, then top with the pimientos. Bake as directed above, or until the crust is crisp and brown. Cut and serve.

Athens Pizza

6 to 8 slices

You'd better get ready for a tasty trip to the Mediterranean... and no, you won't need your passport!

Pizza base of your choice:

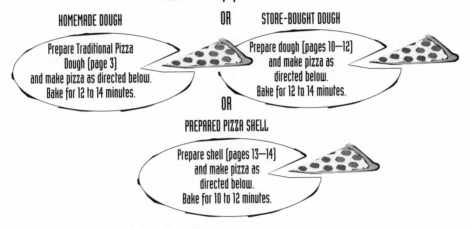

HOMEMADE DOUGH **OR** **STORE-BOUGHT DOUGH**

Prepare Traditional Pizza Dough [page 3] and make pizza as directed below. Bake for 12 to 14 minutes.

Prepare dough [pages 10–12] and make pizza as directed below. Bake for 12 to 14 minutes.

OR

PREPARED PIZZA SHELL

Prepare shell [pages 13–14] and make pizza as directed below. Bake for 10 to 12 minutes.

1 package (10 ounces) frozen chopped spinach, thawed and well drained
4 ounces feta cheese, crumbled (1 cup)

1 cup (8 ounces) cottage cheese, drained
1/4 cup grated Parmesan cheese
1 egg

Preheat the oven to 450°F. If using Traditional Pizza Dough or store-bought dough, bake for 7 to 9 minutes, just until golden. Remove from the oven and set aside. Meanwhile, in a small bowl, combine the remaining ingredients and mix until well blended. Spread the mixture evenly over the crust and bake as directed above, or until the crust is crisp and brown. Cut and serve.

NOTE: If you want to try something a little different with this one, make it with Garlic Dough or Herb Dough (both on page 5).

Good Fortune Pizza

6 to 8 slices

China meets Italy when you create this pizza that will certainly bring you "good fortune"!

Pizza dough of your choice:

HOMEMADE DOUGH   **OR**   **STORE-BOUGHT DOUGH**

Prepare Deep-Dish Pizza Dough (page 6) and make pizza as directed below. Bake for 40 to 45 minutes.

Prepare dough (pages 10–11) and make pizza as directed below. Bake for 40 to 45 minutes.

1 tablespoon peanut oil
1 tablespoon chopped garlic (3 cloves)
3 cups sliced fresh mushrooms (about 8 ounces)
1 medium-sized onion, cut in half and sliced 1/4 inch thick
1 can (8 ounces) sliced water chestnuts, drained

1/2 pound bottom or top round steak, cut into very thin strips
1/2 teaspoon salt
1/2 cup bottled sweet-and-sour sauce
1 tablespoon plus 1 teaspoon soy sauce
1/4 teaspoon cayenne pepper
1 1/2 teaspoons sesame seeds

Preheat the oven to 400°F. In a large skillet, heat the oil over medium-high heat. Add the garlic and sauté for about 1 minute, or just until it begins to brown. Add the mushrooms, onion, and water chestnuts. Cook for 5 to 7 minutes, or until tender. Add the steak and sauté for 2 to 3 minutes, or until no pink remains; drain off the excess liquid. Add the salt and mix well. Remove from the heat. In a small bowl, combine the sweet-and-sour sauce, soy sauce, and cayenne pepper. Add to the beef; mix well to coat. Spoon evenly over the prepared dough. Sprinkle with the sesame seeds. Bake as directed above, or until the crust is crisp and brown. Allow the pizza to sit for a few minutes after removing from the oven, then cut and serve.

Curry Shrimp Pizza

6 to 8 slices

Isn't it time to bring home the tastes of India? You'll be glad you did!

Pizza base of your choice:

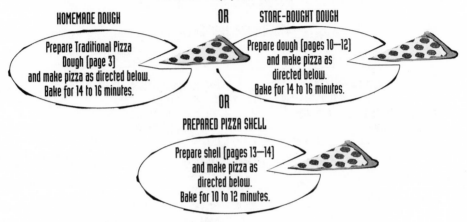

HOMEMADE DOUGH OR **STORE-BOUGHT DOUGH**

Prepare Traditional Pizza Dough (page 3) and make pizza as directed below. Bake for 14 to 16 minutes.

Prepare dough (pages 10–12) and make pizza as directed below. Bake for 14 to 16 minutes.

OR

PREPARED PIZZA SHELL

Prepare shell (pages 13–14) and make pizza as directed below. Bake for 10 to 12 minutes.

1/2 pound medium-sized cooked shrimp, peeled and deveined (20 to 25 shrimp)
1/2 cup mayonnaise
2 1/2 teaspoons curry powder
1/4 teaspoon salt
1/8 teaspoon pepper
1 cup (4 ounces) shredded Monterey Jack cheese
1/4 cup sliced scallions

Preheat the oven to 450°F. If using Traditional Pizza Dough or store-bought dough, bake for 7 to 9 minutes, just until golden. Remove from the oven and set aside. In a large bowl, combine the shrimp, mayonnaise, curry powder, salt, and pepper; mix well. Spread the mixture evenly over the crust and top with the cheese and scallions. Bake as directed above, or until the crust is crisp and brown. Cut and serve.

NOTE: You can use any type of shrimp—canned and drained, frozen and thawed, or cooked fresh. You know I like you to have options!

Chicken Satay Pizza

6 to 8 slices

Hot, spicy chicken and peanuts... Mmm! You won't believe this incredible combination of flavors till you taste it... and then you won't be able to stop eating it!

Pizza base of your choice:

HOMEMADE DOUGH OR **STORE-BOUGHT DOUGH**

Prepare Traditional Pizza Dough [page 3] and make pizza as directed below. Bake for 12 to 14 minutes.

Prepare dough [pages 10–12] and make pizza as directed below. Bake for 12 to 14 minutes.

OR

PREPARED PIZZA SHELL

Prepare shell [pages 13–14] and make pizza as directed below. Bake for 10 to 12 minutes.

½ cup creamy peanut butter
2 tablespoons soy sauce
2 teaspoons sesame oil
1 tablespoon butter
2 teaspoons crushed red pepper

2 cups diced cooked chicken
  (about ½ pound)
¼ cup chopped peanuts
⅓ cup chopped scallions

Preheat the oven to 450°F. In a small saucepan, combine the peanut butter, soy sauce, oil, butter, and red pepper. Cook for 1 to 2 minutes over low heat, until the butter is melted and the mixture is creamy. Remove from the heat and stir in the chicken; mix until well coated. Carefully spread the mixture over the prepared base. Sprinkle with the chopped peanuts and scallions. Bake as directed above, or until the crust is crisp and brown. Cut and serve.

NOTE: If you like it really spicy, then make the Crushed Red Pepper Dough (page 5)…but make sure you've got a way to put out the fire!

Fish 'n' Chips Pizza

6 to 8 slices

In English villages, the fish-and-chips man still comes 'round in his truck to sell his piping-hot dish (just like ice cream vendors here)! You'd better not wait for anyone to deliver fish and chips to *you*, 'cause it'd take a mighty long time... but this recipe doesn't!

Pizza base of your choice:

HOMEMADE DOUGH   **OR**   **STORE-BOUGHT DOUGH**

Prepare Traditional Pizza Dough [page 3] and make pizza as directed below. Bake for 12 to 14 minutes.

Prepare dough [pages 10–12] and make pizza as directed below. Bake for 12 to 14 minutes.

OR

PREPARED PIZZA SHELL

Prepare shell [pages 13–14] and make pizza as directed below. Bake for 10 to 12 minutes.

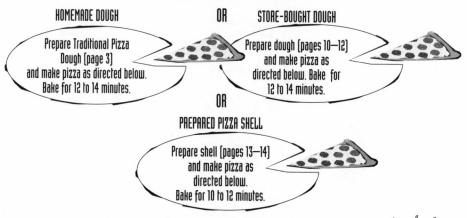

3/4 cup (6 ounces) tartar sauce
1 package (6 to 8 ounces) frozen fish sticks (about 10 fish sticks), thawed and cut into 1/2-inch pieces
1/2 cup crushed potato chips

Preheat the oven to 450°F.
Spread the tartar sauce evenly over the prepared base and top with the fish sticks. Sprinkle the potato chips over the top and bake as directed above, or until the crust is crisp and brown. Cut and serve.

NOTE: Top it off in true British fashion by sprinkling on some malt vinegar.

Israeli Pizza

6 to 8 slices

This is a cool, refreshing pizza that's a perfect go-along for brunch, lunch, or dinner. It's even an ideal snack!

Pizza base of your choice:

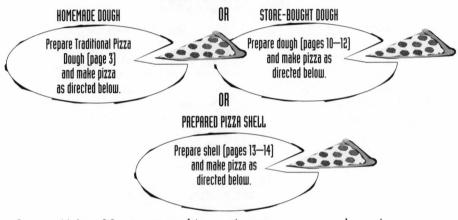

HOMEMADE DOUGH

Prepare Traditional Pizza Dough [page 3] and make pizza as directed below.

OR

STORE-BOUGHT DOUGH

Prepare dough [pages 10–12] and make pizza as directed below.

OR

PREPARED PIZZA SHELL

Prepare shell [pages 13–14] and make pizza as directed below.

2 cans (16 to 20 ounces each) garbanzo beans (chick peas), drained, $1/3$ cup liquid reserved
1 tablespoon chopped garlic (3 cloves)
2 teaspoons fresh lemon juice
3 tablespoons olive oil

1 teaspoon ground cumin
1 teaspoon salt
1 medium-sized tomato, chopped (about $1^1/4$ cups)
1 small cucumber, chopped (about 1 cup)

Preheat the oven to 450°F. If using Traditional Pizza Dough or store-bought dough, bake for 10 to 12 minutes, or until crisp and brown. Remove from the oven and let cool. In a food processor, combine the remaining ingredients except the tomato and cucumber. Process for about 1 minute, until smooth and creamy, scraping down the sides of the bowl as needed. Spread the mixture over the cooled crust and top with the tomato and cucumber. No additional baking is required—just cut and serve.

Caribbean Chicken Pizza

6 to 8 slices

Can you hear the calypso music? This pizza will make you think you're right there, dancing on the beach.

Pizza base of your choice:

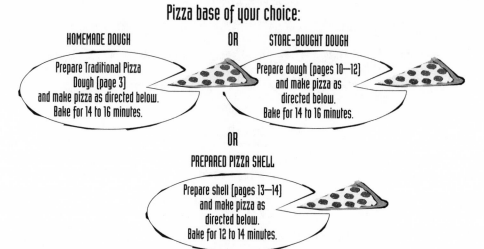

HOMEMADE DOUGH

Prepare Traditional Pizza Dough (page 3) and make pizza as directed below. Bake for 14 to 16 minutes.

OR

STORE-BOUGHT DOUGH

Prepare dough (pages 10–12) and make pizza as directed below. Bake for 14 to 16 minutes.

OR

PREPARED PIZZA SHELL

Prepare shell (pages 13–14) and make pizza as directed below. Bake for 12 to 14 minutes.

1 medium-sized ripe mango, peeled and pitted
¹/₂ cup coarsely chopped red onion (about ¹/₂ a medium-sized onion)
2 tablespoons canned green chilies, drained
1 tablespoon vegetable oil

4 boneless, skinless chicken breast halves (about 1 pound), cut into ¹/₂-inch chunks
2 teaspoons soy sauce
¹/₂ teaspoon ground allspice
1 small red onion, cut into rings

Preheat the oven to 450°F. Place the mango, chopped onion, and chilies in a food processor. Process for 30 seconds, or until the mixture is coarsely chopped. In a large skillet, heat the oil over medium heat. Add the chicken and sauté for 2 to 3 minutes. Add the soy sauce and allspice and cook for 3 to 4 more minutes, or until the chicken is cooked and no pink remains. Add the mango mixture, then reduce the heat to low and simmer for 2 to 3 minutes. Spoon the chicken mixture over the prepared base. Top with the onion rings and bake as directed above, or until the crust is crisp and brown. Cut and serve.

Not-Your-Average Pizzas

If you're hoping for applause when you bring your homemade pizza to the table, make one of these. With their unique look and taste, these are true attention-grabbers.

In this chapter I've taken some of my favorite foods and presented them pizza-style. So if your gang really loves the tastes of a New England clambake, why not surprise them with that perfect combination of corn, potatoes, and tender clams (page 91)? And since Buffalo-style chicken wings are so popular (but so messy!), why not make them on a pizza (page 86) and make no bones about it (or *in* it)? I've even created pizzas with breakfast in mind. Boy, will the kids be happy when you finally let them have pizza for breakfast—Good Morning Pizza with scrambled eggs and bacon (page 75), that is.

These pizzas aren't found on your average pizza menu. Hmm, after thinking about them again, maybe I should have called this chapter Above-Average Pizzas...I bet you'll agree!

Not-Your-Average Pizzas

Ratatouille Pizza

6 to 8 slices

Ratatouille sure has been gaining popularity over the last several years, and when it's served as a pizza topping, you'll find out for yourself why it's a big WOW!

Pizza base of your choice:

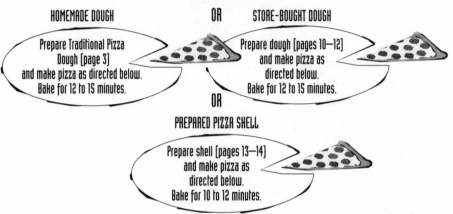

HOMEMADE DOUGH OR **STORE-BOUGHT DOUGH**

Prepare Traditional Pizza Dough (page 3) and make pizza as directed below. Bake for 12 to 15 minutes.

Prepare dough (pages 10–12) and make pizza as directed below. Bake for 12 to 15 minutes.

OR

PREPARED PIZZA SHELL

Prepare shell (pages 13–14) and make pizza as directed below. Bake for 10 to 12 minutes.

¼ cup olive oil
1 small zucchini, cut into ½-inch cubes (about 1½ cups)
½ a medium-sized eggplant, peeled and cut into ½-inch cubes (about 2 cups)
1 medium-sized green bell pepper, cut into ½-inch chunks
8 ounces fresh mushrooms, sliced (about 3 cups)

1 medium-sized onion, coarsely chopped (about 1 cup)
1 can (14½ ounces) whole tomatoes, drained and chopped
2 teaspoons Italian seasoning
1 teaspoon garlic powder
1 teaspoon salt
1 teaspoon black pepper
1 cup (4 ounces) shredded mozzarella cheese

Preheat the oven to 450°F. If using Traditional Pizza Dough or store-bought dough, bake for 7 to 9 minutes, just until golden. Remove from the oven and set aside. In a large skillet, heat the oil over medium heat. Add the zucchini, eggplant, bell pepper, mushrooms, and onion. Cook for 8 to 10 minutes, or until the vegetables are tender, stirring occasionally; drain off the excess liquid. Stir in the remaining ingredients except the cheese. Cook for 4 to 5 minutes, or until all the liquid is absorbed. Spoon the vegetable mixture evenly over the prepared crust and top with the cheese. Bake as directed above, or until the crust is crisp and brown. Cut and serve.

Herbed Chicken
and Red Potato Pizza

6 to 8 slices

You read it right—this is a chicken-and-potato-topped pizza! Oh, I know it sounds fancy, but the combination is "ooh la la!"

Pizza base of your choice:

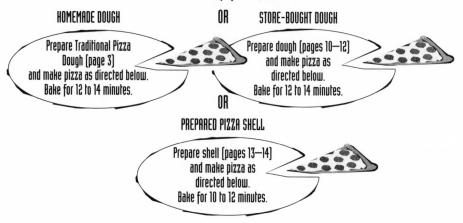

HOMEMADE DOUGH OR **STORE-BOUGHT DOUGH**

Prepare Traditional Pizza Dough [page 3] and make pizza as directed below. Bake for 12 to 14 minutes.

Prepare dough [pages 10–12] and make pizza as directed below. Bake for 12 to 14 minutes.

OR

PREPARED PIZZA SHELL

Prepare shell [pages 13–14] and make pizza as directed below. Bake for 10 to 12 minutes.

1 tablespoon olive oil
1/4 pound small red potatoes (1 to 2 potatoes), sliced 1/8 inch thick
1 teaspoon dried rosemary
1/2 teaspoon dried oregano
1/2 teaspoon dried basil
1/2 teaspoon minced garlic

1/2 teaspoon salt
2 boneless, skinless chicken breast halves (about 1/2 pound), cut into 1/2-inch chunks
1 1/2 cups (6 ounces) shredded white Cheddar cheese, divided

Preheat the oven to 450°F. In a large skillet, heat the oil over medium-low heat. Add the potatoes, herbs, garlic, and salt and sauté for 5 to 7 minutes, or until the potatoes are just tender, stirring occasionally.

Add the chicken and sauté for 5 minutes. Top the prepared base with half of the Cheddar cheese, then spread the chicken and potato mixture over the cheese and top with the remaining cheese. Bake as directed above, or until the crust is crisp and brown. Cut and serve.

Dilly Salmon Pizza

6 to 8 slices

When I first made this, I wondered how it would score when it came out of the oven. Well, I gave it high marks, so see if *you* give it a gold star, too!

Pizza base of your choice:

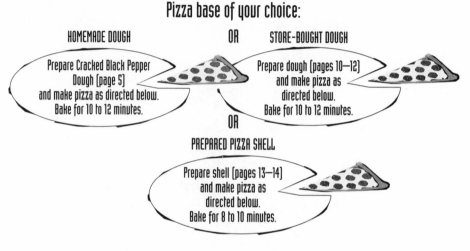

HOMEMADE DOUGH OR **STORE-BOUGHT DOUGH**

Prepare Cracked Black Pepper Dough [page 5] and make pizza as directed below. Bake for 10 to 12 minutes.

Prepare dough [pages 10–12] and make pizza as directed below. Bake for 10 to 12 minutes.

OR

PREPARED PIZZA SHELL

Prepare shell [pages 13–14] and make pizza as directed below. Bake for 8 to 10 minutes.

3/4 cup mayonnaise
1 teaspoon dried dill
1/2 teaspoon dry mustard
1 can (7½ ounces) red or pink
   salmon, drained and flaked

1 cup (4 ounces) shredded
   Havarti cheese

Preheat the oven to 450°F. In a small bowl, combine the mayonnaise, dill, and mustard; mix until blended. Spread evenly over the prepared base. Sprinkle with the salmon and top with the Havarti cheese. Bake as directed above, or until the crust is crisp and brown. Cut and serve.

Good Morning Pizza

6 to 8 slices

A traditional breakfast can be a real hassle to prepare. I mean, timing is everything—between keeping the eggs from getting cold and the toast from burning while the bacon sizzles away. But with a Good Morning Pizza you get to cook it all at once! Give it a shot.

Pizza base of your choice:

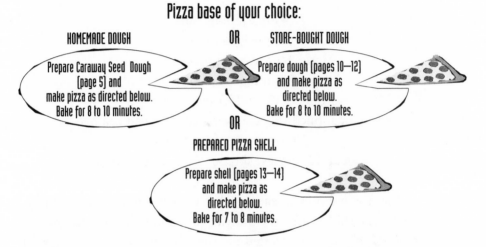

HOMEMADE DOUGH

Prepare Caraway Seed Dough [page 5] and make pizza as directed below. Bake for 8 to 10 minutes.

OR

STORE-BOUGHT DOUGH

Prepare dough [pages 10–12] and make pizza as directed below. Bake for 8 to 10 minutes.

OR

PREPARED PIZZA SHELL

Prepare shell [pages 13–14] and make pizza as directed below. Bake for 7 to 8 minutes.

1 tablespoon butter
6 eggs, beaten
1/3 cup crumbled cooked bacon
   or bacon bits

3 slices American cheese, cut
   into 1/2-inch strips

Preheat the oven to 450°F. If using Caraway Seed Dough or store-bought dough, bake for 7 to 9 minutes, just until golden. Remove from the oven and set aside. In a large skillet, melt the butter over medium-low heat. Add the eggs and scramble until firm but not browned. Spoon the scrambled eggs over the prepared crust and sprinkle with the bacon. Place the strips of cheese over the bacon and bake as directed above, or until the crust is crisp and brown. Cut and serve.

Omelet "Pizza"

6 to 8 slices

Is it an omelet? Is it a frittata? It's an omelet pizza—the fun answer to breakfast. (You have to eat *this* pizza with a fork.)

8 eggs
2 tablespoons milk
$^1/_2$ teaspoon salt
$^1/_4$ teaspoon pepper
2 tablespoons butter
5 ounces ($^1/_2$ a 10-ounce package)
frozen chopped broccoli, thawed and well drained
2 tablespoons bacon bits
$^3/_4$ cup (3 ounces) shredded Cheddar cheese

In a medium-sized bowl, beat together the eggs, milk, salt, and pepper. In a large skillet, melt the butter over medium heat. Add the egg mixture and allow to set around the edges, then use a wooden spoon to push the loose edges slightly toward the center, tilting the pan gently and allowing the liquid to run underneath. Continue to cook for 5 to 6 minutes, pushing the cooked edges in toward the center as necessary, until the eggs are mostly firm. Reduce the heat to medium-low and sprinkle the broccoli over the eggs, then top with the bacon bits and cheese. Cover and cook for 6 to 8 more minutes, or until the cheese is melted and the toppings are hot. Cut into wedges and serve.

NOTE: This can be made 1 to 2 hours in advance, then simply reheated in a 300°F. oven for 10 minutes.

Beefy Garlic Pizza

6 to 8 slices

I've heard that garlic keeps away vampires. Well, it must be working, 'cause I haven't seen a vampire in all the time I've been making this!

Pizza base of your choice:

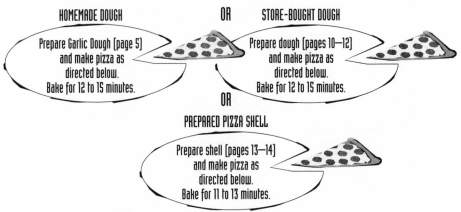

HOMEMADE DOUGH OR **STORE-BOUGHT DOUGH**

Prepare Garlic Dough (page 5) and make pizza as directed below. Bake for 12 to 15 minutes.

Prepare dough (pages 10–12) and make pizza as directed below. Bake for 12 to 15 minutes.

OR

PREPARED PIZZA SHELL

Prepare shell (pages 13–14) and make pizza as directed below. Bake for 11 to 13 minutes.

2 tablespoons vegetable oil
1 bulb of fresh garlic, peeled
  and separated into cloves
  (see Note)
1 pound ground beef
1 cup chopped seeded plum
  tomatoes (2 to 3 tomatoes)

1 teaspoon salt
1 teaspoon pepper
1 package (6 ounces) sliced
  provolone cheese

Preheat the oven to 450°F. In a large skillet, heat the oil over medium-high heat and sauté the garlic for 4 to 5 minutes, until golden brown. Add the ground beef and cook for 8 to 10 minutes, or until completely browned, stirring frequently. Drain off the excess liquid and stir in the tomatoes, salt, and pepper. Spoon the mixture onto the prepared base. Top with the cheese and bake as directed above, or until the crust is crisp and brown. Cut and serve.

NOTE: If the garlic cloves aren't all about the same size, cut the bigger ones in half or in quarters. That way, they'll all cook evenly.

"Feel Like a Kid" Spaghetti Pizza

6 to 8 slices

I hate to admit it, but when I was a kid I often ate cold leftover spaghetti and sauce on white bread. That's why this pizza brings back memories of my childhood! Yup, it makes me "feel like a kid"!

Pizza base of your choice:

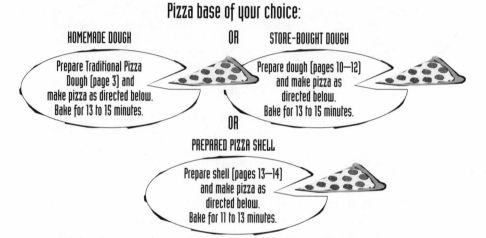

HOMEMADE DOUGH **OR** STORE-BOUGHT DOUGH

Prepare Traditional Pizza Dough [page 3] and make pizza as directed below. Bake for 13 to 15 minutes.

Prepare dough [pages 10–12] and make pizza as directed below. Bake for 13 to 15 minutes.

OR

PREPARED PIZZA SHELL

Prepare shell [pages 13–14] and make pizza as directed below. Bake for 11 to 13 minutes.

2 cups cooked spaghetti (see Note)
1 cup (8 ounces) spaghetti sauce
½ teaspoon crushed red pepper

½ teaspoon dried oregano
1 cup (4 ounces) shredded mozzarella cheese

Preheat the oven to 450°F. In a medium-sized bowl, combine all of the topping ingredients except the cheese; mix well. Spoon evenly onto the prepared base. Top with the mozzarella cheese and bake as directed above, or until the crust is crisp and brown. Cut and serve.

NOTE: You'll need 4 ounces of uncooked spaghetti prepared according to the package directions to make 2 cups cooked spaghetti. Of course, this is just the thing to make if you've got leftover spaghetti.

Gazpacho Pizza

6 to 8 slices

I couldn't decide whether to name this Minestrone Pizza or Gazpacho Pizza. After you make it, you'll know why it was a tough call.

Pizza base of your choice:

HOMEMADE DOUGH

Prepare Traditional Pizza Dough [page 3] and make pizza as directed below. Bake for 10 to 12 minutes.

OR

STORE-BOUGHT DOUGH

Prepare dough [pages 10–12] and make pizza as directed below. Bake for 10 to 12 minutes.

OR

PREPARED PIZZA SHELL

Prepare shell [pages 13–14] and make pizza as directed below. Bake for 10 to 12 minutes.

1 package (10 ounces) frozen mixed vegetables, thawed and drained
1 jar (11.5 ounces) salsa, well drained

1 medium-sized tomato, chopped (about 1¼ cups)
1 cup (4 ounces) shredded Mexican blend cheese

Preheat the oven to 450°F. If using Traditional Pizza Dough or store-bought dough, bake for 7 to 9 minutes, just until golden. Remove from the oven and set aside. In a medium-sized bowl, combine the mixed vegetables and salsa; mix until blended. Spread evenly over the prepared crust, then sprinkle with the chopped tomato and top with the cheese. Bake as directed above, or until the crust is crisp and brown. Cut and serve.

NOTE: Hot, medium, or mild—choose whichever type of salsa you prefer. Remember, all salsas are *not* created equal!

Veal Oscar Pizza

6 to 8 slices

Sometimes pizza can become a little bit more, shall I say, "fancy" with the right toppings, but without extra work. This is a perfect example.

Pizza dough of your choice:

HOMEMADE DOUGH   OR   **STORE-BOUGHT DOUGH**

Prepare Deep-Dish Pizza Dough (page 6) and make pizza as directed below. Bake for 30 to 35 minutes.

Prepare dough (pages 10–11) and make pizza as directed below. Bake for 30 to 35 minutes.

1 pound ground veal	1 package (10 ounces) frozen
1/2 teaspoon salt	cut asparagus, thawed and
1/4 teaspoon pepper	drained
1/2 cup chopped imitation	1 cup (4 ounces) shredded mild
crabmeat (about 4 ounces)	Cheddar cheese

Preheat the oven to 400°F. In a medium-sized skillet, brown the veal over medium heat for 8 to 10 minutes until no pink remains. Remove from the heat and drain off the excess liquid. Stir in the salt and pepper and spread evenly over the prepared dough. Top with the crabmeat, asparagus, and cheese. Bake as directed above, or until the crust is crisp and brown. Cut and serve.

NOTE: You can substitute cooked shrimp for the crab if you prefer.

Roasted Pepper Pizza

6 to 8 slices

Wanna look gourmet-fancy without all the work? This recipe's for you.

Pizza base of your choice:

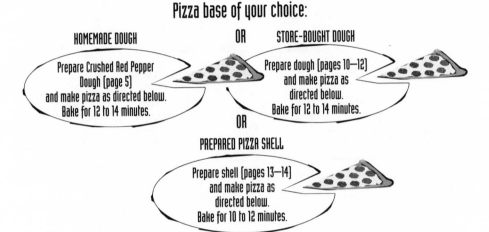

HOMEMADE DOUGH OR **STORE-BOUGHT DOUGH**

Prepare Crushed Red Pepper Dough [page 5] and make pizza as directed below. Bake for 12 to 14 minutes.

Prepare dough [pages 10–12] and make pizza as directed below. Bake for 12 to 14 minutes.

OR

PREPARED PIZZA SHELL

Prepare shell [pages 13–14] and make pizza as directed below. Bake for 10 to 12 minutes.

1 jar (7.5 ounces) roasted peppers, drained and cut into 1/4-inch slices
8 ounces feta cheese, crumbled (about 1 1/2 cups)

1 tablespoon chopped garlic (3 cloves)

Preheat the oven to 450°F. Place the roasted pepper strips evenly over the prepared base. In a small bowl, combine the cheese and garlic. Sprinkle the cheese mixture over the peppers and bake as directed above, or until the crust is crisp and brown. Cut and serve.

Chicken and Roasted Garlic Pizza

6 to 8 slices

Oh! There's an ingredient missing here…I didn't list it, but I do recommend it. Yup, it's breath mints!

Pizza dough of your choice:

HOMEMADE DOUGH   OR   **STORE-BOUGHT DOUGH**

Prepare Deep-Dish Pizza Dough (page 6) and make pizza as directed below. Bake for 40 to 45 minutes.

Prepare dough (pages 10–11) and make pizza as directed below. Bake for 40 to 45 minutes.

1 bulb roasted garlic (see page 19)
1 tablespoon olive oil
2 boneless, skinless chicken breast halves (about ¹/₂ pound), cut into ¹/₂-inch cubes

1 teaspoon salt
¹/₂ teaspoon pepper
3 medium-sized plum tomatoes, sliced ¹/₄ inch thick
1 cup (4 ounces) shredded mozzarella cheese

Preheat the oven to 400°F. Remove the roasted garlic from the skin and spread over the prepared dough. In a small skillet, heat the oil over medium-high heat. Sauté the chicken for 4 to 5 minutes, or just until no pink remains, stirring occasionally; do not overcook. Drain off the excess liquid, then stir in the salt and pepper. Spoon the chicken evenly over the roasted garlic; top with the tomatoes, then the cheese. Bake as directed above, or until the crust is crisp and brown. Cut and serve.

NOTE: How 'bout adding herbs to the Deep-Dish Pizza Dough (page 5)? It's delicious!

Mixed Olive Pizza

6 to 8 slices

Cross-cultural cooking is really popular these days, and it's ever-so-tasty in this blending of Greek and Italian ideas.

Pizza base of your choice:

HOMEMADE DOUGH   OR   **STORE-BOUGHT DOUGH**

Prepare Traditional Pizza Dough [page 3] and make pizza as directed below. Bake for 14 to 16 minutes.

Prepare dough [pages 10–12] and make pizza as directed below. Bake for 14 to 16 minutes.

OR

PREPARED PIZZA SHELL

Prepare shell [pages 13–14] and make pizza as directed below. Bake for 12 to 14 minutes.

1/3 cup pizza or spaghetti sauce
1 can (2.25 ounces) sliced black olives, drained (about 1/2 cup)
1/4 cup salad-style pitted green olives, drained

8 ounces feta cheese, crumbled (about 1 1/2 cups)

Preheat the oven to 450°F. Spread the sauce evenly over the prepared base. Sprinkle the olives evenly over the sauce, then top with the feta cheese. Bake as directed above, or until the crust is crisp and brown. Cut and serve.

NOTE: For real homemade taste, I suggest using Spicy Chunky Pizza Sauce (page 15). I use salad-style olives because, since they're in pieces, they're less expensive than whole pimiento-stuffed green olives. (Yup, they're the same thing.)

Chicken Caesar Pizza

6 to 8 slices

Your friends will be crying "Hail, Caesar!" after they taste his fantastic namesake pizza.

Pizza base of your choice:

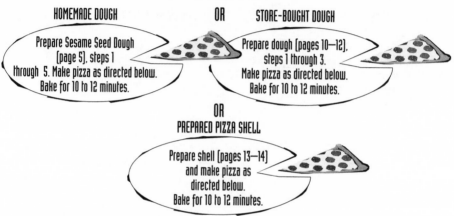

HOMEMADE DOUGH

Prepare Sesame Seed Dough [page 5], steps 1 through 5. Make pizza as directed below. Bake for 10 to 12 minutes.

OR

STORE-BOUGHT DOUGH

Prepare dough [pages 10–12], steps 1 through 3. Make pizza as directed below. Bake for 10 to 12 minutes.

OR

PREPARED PIZZA SHELL

Prepare shell [pages 13–14] and make pizza as directed below. Bake for 10 to 12 minutes.

1 tablespoon olive oil
1 tablespoon chopped garlic (about 3 cloves)
2 boneless, skinless chicken breast halves (about 1/2 pound), cut into 3/4-inch chunks
1/2 teaspoon ground dried rosemary
1 can (about 2 ounces) anchovy fillets, drained and coarsely chopped

3 artichoke hearts (about 1/2 a 14-ounce can), drained and coarsely chopped
1/3 cup Caesar salad dressing (not creamy-style), divided
1 cup grated Parmesan cheese, divided
2 cups coarsely chopped romaine lettuce

Preheat the oven to 450°F. In a medium-sized skillet, heat the oil over medium heat. Sauté the garlic for 1 minute, just until it begins to brown. Reduce the heat to medium-low and add the chicken and rosemary. Cook, stirring, for 5 to 7 minutes, or until no pink remains. Add the anchovies, artichoke hearts, and 2 tablespoons of the dressing. Stir until well blended and remove from the heat. Spread 1 tablespoon of the dressing over the prepared base, then sprinkle with ¾ cup of the Parmesan cheese. Spread the chicken mixture over the cheese and bake as directed above, or until the crust is crisp and brown. Meanwhile, in a medium-sized bowl, toss the romaine with the remaining dressing and Parmesan cheese. Remove the pizza from the oven and top with the salad mix. Cut and serve.

Buffalo Chicken Pizza

6 to 8 slices

So many pizzerias offer chicken wings on their menus now. We can do them one better by putting the Buffalo-style chicken-wing flavor right on the pizza!

Pizza base of your choice:

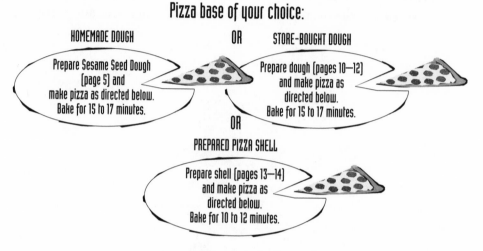

HOMEMADE DOUGH

Prepare Sesame Seed Dough
(page 5) and
make pizza as directed below.
Bake for 15 to 17 minutes.

OR

STORE-BOUGHT DOUGH

Prepare dough (pages 10–12)
and make pizza as
directed below.
Bake for 15 to 17 minutes.

OR

PREPARED PIZZA SHELL

Prepare shell (pages 13–14)
and make pizza as
directed below.
Bake for 10 to 12 minutes.

¼ cup (½ stick) butter, melted
¼ cup hot cayenne pepper
   sauce
2 cups diced cooked chicken
   (about ½ pound)

½ cup chopped celery
4 ounces blue cheese, crumbled
   (1 cup)

Preheat the oven to 450°F. In a medium-sized bowl, combine the butter and hot pepper sauce; mix well. Add the chicken and celery and toss to coat well. Spread evenly over the prepared base, then sprinkle with the blue cheese. Bake as directed above, or until the crust is crisp and brown. Cut and serve.

NOTE: Are you daring? You can increase the amount of hot cayenne pepper sauce to ⅓ cup—but watch out!

Crabmeat and Pesto Pizza

6 to 8 slices

Four ingredients on a pizza crust can create a really big taste...find out for yourself.

Pizza base of your choice:

HOMEMADE DOUGH

Prepare Traditional Pizza Dough [page 3] and make pizza as directed below. Bake for 13 to 15 minutes.

OR

STORE-BOUGHT DOUGH

Prepare dough [pages 10–12] and make pizza as directed below. Bake for 13 to 15 minutes.

OR

PREPARED PIZZA SHELL

Prepare shell [pages 13–14] and make pizza as directed below. Bake for 12 to 14 minutes.

½ cup White Pizza Sauce (page 17)
2 tablespoons Homemade Pesto Sauce (page 18) or prepared pesto

1½ cups flaked imitation crabmeat (about 6 ounces)
1 cup (4 ounces) shredded Havarti cheese

Preheat the oven to 450°F. In a small bowl, combine the sauces; mix well. Spread evenly over the prepared base. Sprinkle evenly with the crabmeat, then top with the cheese. Bake as directed above, or until the crust is crisp and brown. Cut and serve.

NOTE: This is a super luncheon pizza. Or why not cut it into 2-inch squares and serve it as an hors d'oeuvre...that's easy, too!

Eggplant Parmigiana Pizza

6 to 8 slices

Eggplant parmigiana is such a classic dish that I was almost afraid to do anything different with it. But I decided to try it as a pizza topping, and am I glad I did! It just added to its goodness!

Pizza base of your choice:

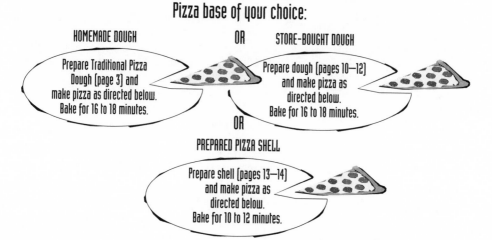

HOMEMADE DOUGH

Prepare Traditional Pizza Dough (page 3) and make pizza as directed below. Bake for 16 to 18 minutes.

OR

STORE-BOUGHT DOUGH

Prepare dough (pages 10–12) and make pizza as directed below. Bake for 16 to 18 minutes.

OR

PREPARED PIZZA SHELL

Prepare shell (pages 13–14) and make pizza as directed below. Bake for 10 to 12 minutes.

1 egg
1/4 cup milk
1/4 teaspoon salt
1/2 a medium-sized eggplant (about 1/2 pound), peeled and cut into 1/4-inch slices
3/4 cup seasoned bread crumbs
1/4 teaspoon dried oregano
1/4 teaspoon garlic powder
1/4 cup plus 1 tablespoon grated Parmesan cheese, divided
1/4 cup plus 2 tablespoons olive oil, divided
2/3 cup pizza or spaghetti sauce
1 1/2 cups (6 ounces) shredded mozzarella cheese

Preheat the oven to 450°F. In a medium-sized bowl, beat together the egg, milk, and salt. Add the eggplant and toss to coat. In another medium-sized bowl, combine the bread crumbs, oregano, garlic powder, and 1 tablespoon of the Parmesan cheese. In a large skillet, heat 3 tablespoons of the oil over medium heat. Dip the eggplant into the bread crumb mixture, coating well, then fill the hot skillet with eggplant. Cook for 3 to 5 minutes on each side, or until the breading is golden. Lay on paper towels to drain. Add the remaining 3 tablespoons oil to the skillet and, when hot, cook the remaining eggplant. Spread the sauce evenly over the prepared base and sprinkle with the remaining 1/4 cup Parmesan cheese. Arrange the cooked eggplant in a single layer on the Parmesan and top with the mozzarella cheese. Bake as directed above, or until the crust is crisp and brown. Cut and serve.

NOTE: Be careful when frying the eggplant because the oil will be very hot. If the oil begins to burn, reduce the heat and remove the skillet from the burner until it's cooled enough to fry again.

Black Bean Pizza

6 to 8 slices

C'mon, you can have this ready in minutes. And black beans are so good for us that this'll surely make you an instant hero!

Pizza base of your choice:

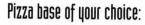

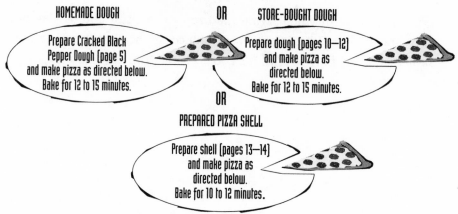

HOMEMADE DOUGH

Prepare Cracked Black Pepper Dough [page 5] and make pizza as directed below. Bake for 12 to 15 minutes.

OR

STORE-BOUGHT DOUGH

Prepare dough [pages 10–12] and make pizza as directed below. Bake for 12 to 15 minutes.

OR

PREPARED PIZZA SHELL

Prepare shell [pages 13–14] and make pizza as directed below. Bake for 10 to 12 minutes.

1 jar (16 ounces) salsa, drained
⅓ cup pizza or spaghetti sauce
1 can (15 ounces) black beans, rinsed and drained

1 cup (4 ounces) shredded Cheddar cheese

Preheat the oven to 450°F. In a medium-sized bowl, combine the salsa and pizza sauce. Spread evenly over the prepared base. Spoon the black beans over the sauce, then top with the cheese. Bake as directed above, or until the crust is crisp and brown. Cut and serve.

Clambake Pizza

6 to 8 slices

We've all heard of New England clambakes overflowing with chowder, clams, and corn on the cob. Well, if we join those tastes on a pizza crust, the only thing missing will be the Atlantic Ocean.

Pizza base of your choice:

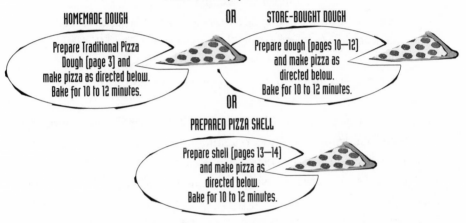

HOMEMADE DOUGH **OR** STORE-BOUGHT DOUGH

Prepare Traditional Pizza Dough (page 3) and make pizza as directed below. Bake for 10 to 12 minutes.

Prepare dough (pages 10–12) and make pizza as directed below. Bake for 10 to 12 minutes.

OR

PREPARED PIZZA SHELL

Prepare shell (pages 13–14) and make pizza as directed below. Bake for 10 to 12 minutes.

1 can (10¾ ounces) condensed New England clam chowder
1 can (6.5 ounces) chopped clams, drained
1 can (8 ounces) whole kernel corn, drained

½ cup sour cream
1 cup (4 ounces) shredded Monterey Jack cheese

Preheat the oven to 450°F. If using Traditional Pizza Dough or store-bought dough, bake for 7 to 9 minutes, just until golden. Remove from the oven and set aside. In a medium-sized bowl, combine the clam chowder, clams, corn, and sour cream; mix until well blended. Spread the clam mixture over the prepared crust and top with the cheese. Bake as directed above, or until the crust is crisp and brown. Cut and serve.

Covered Lasagna Pizza

6 to 8 slices

This sure isn't a traditional pizza...nope, not even a traditional crust. The secret is in the lasagna noodles—they're the crust. Just wait till you serve your family *this* pizza!

12 uncooked lasagna noodles
3 cups (12 ounces) shredded mozzarella cheese, divided
1 package (3½ ounces) sliced pepperoni (about 50 slices)
1½ cups sliced fresh mushrooms
1 jar (14 ounces) pizza or spaghetti sauce (1¾ cups)

Preheat the oven to 375°F. Cook the noodles according to the package directions; drain, rinse, drain again, and pat dry with paper towels. Place 6 lasagna noodles crosswise on a 10" × 15" rimmed cookie sheet that has been coated with nonstick vegetable spray. (Cut the noodles to fit, if necessary.) Sprinkle 1¼ cups of the cheese over the noodles. Layer the pepperoni, then the mushrooms, evenly over the cheese. Cover with the remaining noodles, placed in the same crosswise direction. Spread the sauce over the noodles and sprinkle with the remaining 1¾ cups cheese. Coat one side of a large piece of aluminum foil with nonstick vegetable spray and cover the pan (with the coated side down so the cheese won't stick). Bake for 20 minutes, or until the cheese is melted. Let sit for 8 to 10 minutes, then cut and serve.

Hearty Artichoke and Pesto Pizza

6 to 8 slices

Garden fresh? Yup. Impressive? You bet. Easy to make? Yes, yes, yes!

Pizza base of your choice:

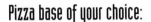

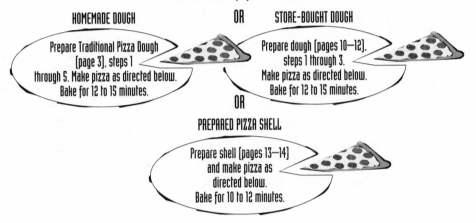

HOMEMADE DOUGH   **OR**   **STORE-BOUGHT DOUGH**

Prepare Traditional Pizza Dough [page 3], steps 1 through 5. Make pizza as directed below. Bake for 12 to 15 minutes.

Prepare dough [pages 10–12], steps 1 through 3. Make pizza as directed below. Bake for 12 to 15 minutes.

OR

PREPARED PIZZA SHELL

Prepare shell [pages 13–14] and make pizza as directed below. Bake for 10 to 12 minutes.

½ cup Homemade Pesto Sauce (page 18) or prepared pesto
1 can (14 ounces) artichoke hearts, drained and quartered

4 ounces fresh mozzarella cheese (like buffalo), sliced about ¼ inch thick

Preheat the oven to 450°F. Spread the pesto sauce evenly over the prepared base, then scatter the artichoke hearts over the sauce. Cover with the cheese and bake as directed above, or until the crust is crisp and brown. Cut and serve.

Fire Department Chili Pizza

6 to 8 slices

Chili cook-offs are being held everywhere now, but you won't have to bother entering one. Know why? 'Cause you'll have the award-winning taste of chili pizza right there at home.

Pizza dough of your choice:

HOMEMADE DOUGH   **OR**   **STORE-BOUGHT DOUGH**

Prepare Deep-Dish Pizza Dough (page 6) and make pizza as directed below. Bake for 35 to 40 minutes.

Prepare dough (pages 10—11) and make pizza as directed below. Bake for 35 to 40 minutes.

1 can (15 ounces) prepared chili (with meat)
1 medium-sized onion, chopped (about 1 cup)

1 cup (4 ounces) shredded Cheddar cheese

Preheat the oven to 400°F. Spread the chili evenly over the prepared dough and sprinkle with the onion. Top with the cheese and bake as directed above, or until the crust is crisp and brown. Cut and serve.

NOTE: Why not use 2 cups of your favorite chili in place of the canned chili? Then you can really give 'em a 4-alarm pizza!

Snappy Clam Pizza

6 to 8 slices

Clams and spicy tomato sauce? It's a combination you'll really "dig"!

Pizza base of your choice:

HOMEMADE DOUGH OR **STORE-BOUGHT DOUGH**

Prepare Traditional Pizza Dough (page 3) and make pizza as directed below. Bake for 14 to 16 minutes.

Prepare dough (pages 10–12) and make pizza as directed below. Bake for 14 to 16 minutes.

OR

PREPARED PIZZA SHELL

Prepare shell (pages 13–14) and make pizza as directed below. Bake for 12 to 14 minutes.

1 teaspoon vegetable oil
1 tablespoon chopped garlic (3 cloves)
1 can (10 ounces) whole baby clams, drained

3/4 cup Spicy Chunky Pizza Sauce (page 15)
2 teaspoons chopped fresh parsley or 1 teaspoon dried parsley flakes

Preheat the oven to 450°F. In a medium-sized skillet, heat the oil over medium heat. Add the garlic and sauté for 1 to 2 minutes, until it just begins to brown. Remove from the heat and add the clams and sauce; mix well. Spread the mixture over the prepared base and bake as directed above, or until the crust is crisp and brown. Sprinkle with the parsley, then cut and serve.

NOTE: Don't feel like making Spicy Chunky Pizza Sauce? No problem. Just use a mixture of 1/4 cup spaghetti sauce and 1/2 cup salsa. Easy, huh?

Barbecued Chicken Pizza

6 to 8 slices

Let's keep the taste of barbecued chicken around all year with this lip-smackin' barbecued pizza!

Pizza base of your choice:

| HOMEMADE DOUGH | OR | PREPARED PIZZA SHELL |

Prepare Cornmeal Dough [page 5] and make pizza as directed below. Bake for 13 to 15 minutes.

Prepare shell [pages 13–14] and make pizza as directed below. Bake for 10 to 12 minutes.

1 tablespoon olive oil
4 boneless, skinless chicken breast halves (about 1 pound), cut into 1-inch chunks

½ teaspoon salt
½ cup (4 ounces) barbecue sauce
1 cup (4 ounces) shredded white Cheddar cheese

Preheat the oven to 450°F. In a large skillet, heat the oil over medium heat. Add the chicken, sprinkle with the salt, and sauté for 5 to 7 minutes, or until the chicken is cooked through and no pink remains; drain off the excess liquid. Remove from the heat and add the barbecue sauce; mix until well coated. Spoon evenly over the prepared base. Sprinkle with the cheese. Bake as directed above, or until the crust is crisp and brown. Cut and serve.

Shrimp and Pesto Pizza

6 to 8 slices

Everyone's heard of shrimp cocktails and shrimp scampi, and I think it won't be long before shrimp and pesto are a combination that's just as popular!

Pizza base of your choice:

HOMEMADE DOUGH   OR   **STORE-BOUGHT DOUGH**

Prepare Traditional Pizza Dough [page 3], steps 1 through 5. Make pizza as directed below. Bake for 12 to 15 minutes.

Prepare dough [pages 10–12], steps 1 through 3. Make pizza as directed below. Bake for 12 to 15 minutes.

OR

PREPARED PIZZA SHELL

Prepare shell [pages 13–14] and make pizza as directed below. Bake for 12 to 15 minutes.

¹/₃ cup Homemade Pesto Sauce (page 18) or prepared pesto
4 plum tomatoes, very thinly sliced crosswise

¹/₂ pound medium-sized cooked shrimp (20 to 25 shrimp), peeled and deveined
¹/₂ cup grated Parmesan cheese

Preheat the oven to 450°F. Spread the pesto sauce evenly over the prepared base and cover evenly with the tomato slices. Top with the shrimp, then sprinkle with the Parmesan cheese. Bake as directed above, or until the crust is crisp and brown. Cut and serve.

NOTE: You can use fresh or frozen (thawed) shrimp.

Hickory-Barbecued Beef Pizza

6 to 8 slices

We all have a favorite restaurant that specializes in the great taste of barbecue, but for those times when we want to have our barbecue at home, this pizza can make us think we're standing in front of an open pit, taking in that delicious hickory aroma.

Pizza base of your choice:

HOMEMADE DOUGH   **OR**   **STORE-BOUGHT DOUGH**

Prepare Traditional Pizza Dough (page 3) and make pizza as directed below. Bake for 10 to 12 minutes.

Prepare dough (pages 10–12) and make pizza as directed below. Bake for 10 to 12 minutes.

OR

PREPARED PIZZA SHELL

Prepare shell (pages 13–14) and make pizza as directed below. Bake for 8 to 10 minutes.

¾ pound sliced deli roast beef, cut into 1-inch strips
½ cup (4 ounces) hickory-flavored barbecue sauce

1 cup (4 ounces) shredded smoked Jarlsberg cheese
¼ cup chopped scallions

Preheat the oven to 450°F. If using Traditional Pizza Dough or store-bought dough, bake for 7 to 9 minutes, just until golden. Remove from the oven and set aside. In a large bowl, combine the roast beef and barbecue sauce; mix until well coated. Spoon over the prepared crust and top with the cheese. Bake as directed above, or until the crust is crisp and brown. Remove from the oven and sprinkle with the scallions. Cut and serve.

NOTE: I think hickory-flavored sauce really adds to the taste of this recipe, but if you prefer, substitute your favorite barbecue sauce.

Franks 'n' Beans Pizza

6 to 8 slices

Let's be "frank"—this was my granddaughter's idea. She thinks the results are "hot diggity dog"... and so will you!

Pizza base of your choice:

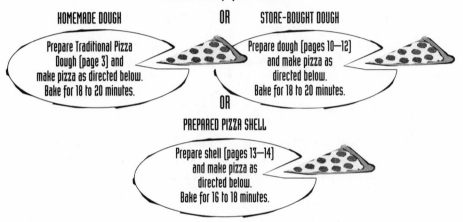

HOMEMADE DOUGH

Prepare Traditional Pizza Dough [page 3] and make pizza as directed below. Bake for 18 to 20 minutes.

OR

STORE-BOUGHT DOUGH

Prepare dough [pages 10–12] and make pizza as directed below. Bake for 18 to 20 minutes.

OR

PREPARED PIZZA SHELL

Prepare shell [pages 13–14] and make pizza as directed below. Bake for 16 to 18 minutes.

1 can (16 ounces) baked beans, drained
1 small onion, chopped (about 1/2 cup)

1/2 pound hot dogs (3 to 5 hot dogs), cut into 1/4-inch slices
1 cup (4 ounces) shredded Cheddar cheese

Preheat the oven to 450°F. In a large bowl, combine the beans, onion, and hot dogs; mix well. Spread over the prepared base and top with the cheese. Bake as directed above, or until the crust is crisp and brown. Cut and serve.

NOTE: Sure, you can try this with chicken or turkey hot dogs and low-fat Cheddar cheese for a lower-fat version.

Sunshine Pizza

6 to 8 slices

Since some days you can feel kind of "blah," I've got a pizza that'll bring a little sunshine into your kitchen.

Pizza base of your choice:

HOMEMADE DOUGH   OR   PREPARED PIZZA SHELL

Prepare Quick Pizza Dough (page 7) and make pizza as directed below. Bake for 15 to 18 minutes.

Prepare shell (pages 13–14) and make pizza as directed below. Bake for 13 to 15 minutes.

1 ounce sun-dried tomatoes (not oil-packed), chopped
1 cup White Pizza Sauce (page 17)

1 can (14 ounces) artichoke hearts, drained, quartered, and patted dry

Preheat the oven to 450°F. Soak the sun-dried tomatoes in warm water for 5 minutes, then drain. Spread the sauce evenly over the prepared base. Arrange the tomatoes in the center of the prepared dough, forming a 5-inch-wide circle to make the center of the pizza "sun." Place the artichoke hearts in lines coming out from the circle, forming the "rays." Bake as directed above, or until the crust is crisp and brown. Cut and serve.

Spicy Mushroom Pizza

6 to 8 slices

Why not add a little pizzazz to your regular mushroom pizza? Go ahead—it's in the cheese!

Pizza base of your choice:

HOMEMADE DOUGH   OR   STORE-BOUGHT DOUGH

Prepare Traditional Pizza Dough (page 3) and make pizza as directed below. Bake for 16 to 18 minutes.

Prepare dough (pages 10–12) and make pizza as directed below. Bake for 16 to 18 minutes.

OR

PREPARED PIZZA SHELL

Prepare shell (pages 13–14) and make pizza as directed below. Bake for 10 to 12 minutes.

2 tablespoons olive oil
1 pound fresh mushrooms, cut in half or into 1/4-inch slices (about 5 cups)
1 teaspoon garlic powder

1/2 teaspoon salt
1/2 cup pizza or spaghetti sauce
1 cup (4 ounces) shredded Monterey Jack pepper cheese

Preheat the oven to 450°F. In a large skillet, heat the oil over medium heat and sauté the mushrooms for 6 to 8 minutes, or just until softened; drain off the excess liquid. Stir in the garlic powder and salt. Spread the sauce evenly over the prepared base and then spread the mushrooms evenly on top. Sprinkle with the cheese. Bake as directed above, or until the crust is crisp and brown. Cut and serve.

NOTE: Monterey Jack pepper cheese is mild Monterey Jack cheese (that's perfect for topping pizza) studded with chopped jalapeño peppers. If you can't find this particular one, try any of the cheeses that have crushed red pepper or chopped jalapeños in them. They'll all give the pizza the same big taste.

Stuffed Pizzas and Calzones

Does your gang ever complain that pizza doesn't fill them up—that those thin slices of delivered pizza just don't satisfy their hunger? These sure will!

Here's a chapter full of pizzas that'll harness the heartiest of appetites. I've got stuffed pizzas, which are two crusts with filling in between, and calzones, which are sort of like stuffed savory turnovers. Both are designed for fillings that need a bit more containment than usual pizza toppings. These are the stick-to-your-ribs pizzas, or, shall I say, the "forget the dessert" pizzas. And are they flavorful! With fillings like veal parmigiana (page 106), chicken pesto (page 115), and spinach and ricotta cheese (page 116) bursting from the rich crusts, I'll bet you'll have a hard time deciding which stuffed favorite you'll want to try first. (But I can guarantee that any one you choose will be an appetite-beater!)

Stuffed Pizzas and Calzones

Stuffed Veal Parmigiana Pizza

6 to 8 slices

If you're a veal parmigiana fan, then this is the pizza for you! It has big Italian taste, and your friends and family will be begging you to make it over and over.

Pizza dough of your choice:

2 BATCHES HOMEMADE DOUGH OR **2 BATCHES STORE-BOUGHT DOUGH**

Prepare 2 batches Traditional Pizza Dough [page 3], steps 1 through 4. Make pizza as directed below.

Prepare 2 batches dough [pages 10–12], steps 1 and 2. Make pizza as directed below.

1 pound ground veal
1 medium-sized onion, chopped (about 1 cup)
1 tablespoon plus 1 teaspoon chopped garlic (4 cloves)
1 cup pizza or spaghetti sauce
1/2 cup grated Parmesan cheese

1/2 teaspoon dried oregano
1/2 teaspoon salt
1/2 teaspoon pepper
1 cup (4 ounces) shredded mozzarella cheese
1 tablespoon olive oil

Preheat the oven to 375°F. In a large nonstick skillet, brown the veal over medium-high heat for 4 to 5 minutes, or until no pink remains. Drain off the excess liquid, then add the onion and garlic. Sauté for 4 to 6 minutes, or until the onion is tender. Reduce the heat to low and add the sauce, Parmesan cheese, oregano, salt, and pepper; mix thoroughly. Spread the mixture evenly onto one of the rounds of dough, leaving a 1-inch border all around. Sprinkle with the mozzarella cheese. Remove the second dough from the pizza pan and place it over the filling. Bring the edge of the bottom dough up over the edge of the top dough. With your fingers or a fork, pinch the edges together firmly to seal. Brush the top with the oil and pierce 3 or 4 times with a fork or knife. Bake for 35 to 40 minutes, or until the crust is crisp and brown. Cut and serve.

Polish Pierogi-Stuffed Pizza

6 to 8 slices

Wow! What a neat side dish this is! It's a really unusual and delicious way to serve potatoes. You're gonna have them coming back for seconds and thirds!

Pizza dough of your choice:

2 BATCHES HOMEMADE DOUGH   OR   **2 BATCHES STORE-BOUGHT DOUGH**

Prepare 2 batches Traditional Pizza Dough (page 3), steps 1 through 4. Make pizza as directed below.

Prepare 2 batches dough (pages 10–12), steps 1 and 2. Make pizza as directed below.

¹/₄ cup vegetable oil
1 medium-sized onion, chopped
  (about 1 cup)
6 servings warm seasoned
  instant mashed potatoes,
  prepared according to the
  package directions

1 cup (4 ounces) shredded
  Cheddar cheese
¹/₄ teaspoon pepper
1 tablespoon olive oil

Preheat the oven to 375°F. In a medium-sized skillet, heat the vegetable oil over medium-high heat and sauté the onion for 10 to 12 minutes, until golden brown; remove from the heat. In a large bowl, combine the potatoes, cheese, pepper, and sautéed onions; mix well. Spread evenly over one of the rounds of dough, leaving a 1-inch border all around. Remove the second dough from the pizza pan and place it over the potato mixture. Bring the edge of the bottom dough up over the edge of the top dough. With your fingers or a fork, pinch the edges together firmly to seal. Brush the top with the olive oil and pierce 3 or 4 times with a fork or knife. Bake for 35 to 40 minutes, or until the crust is crisp and brown. Cut and serve.

NOTE: You can substitute 3 cups of seasoned homemade mashed potatoes for the instant potatoes.

Stuffed Steak Pizza

6 to 8 slices

When the crowd is really hungry and wants something to sink their teeth into, you'll have just the answer.

Pizza dough of your choice:

2 BATCHES HOMEMADE DOUGH OR **2 BATCHES STORE-BOUGHT DOUGH**

Prepare 2 batches Traditional Pizza Dough (page 3), steps 1 through 4. Make pizza as directed below.

Prepare 2 batches dough (pages 10–12), steps 1 and 2. Make pizza as directed below.

2 tablespoons olive oil, divided
1 teaspoon chopped garlic (1 clove)
$^3/_4$ pound beef flank steak, cut into 1-inch cubes
1 large onion, coarsely chopped (about $1^1/_4$ cups)

$^1/_2$ cup (about $^1/_2$ a $10^1/_4$-ounce can) beef gravy
$^1/_2$ teaspoon dried thyme
$^1/_4$ teaspoon pepper
1 cup (4 ounces) shredded Swiss cheese

Preheat the oven to 400°F. In a medium-sized skillet, heat 1 table-spoon of the oil over medium-high heat. Add the garlic and sauté for about 1 minute, or until it just begins to turn golden. Add the steak and onion and cook for 6 to 8 minutes, or until very little pink remains in the meat. Remove from the heat and drain off the excess liquid. Stir in the gravy, thyme, and pepper; mix well. Spread the beef mixture evenly onto one of the rounds of dough, leaving a 1-inch border all around. Remove the second dough from the pizza pan and place it over the beef mixture. Bring the edge of the bottom dough up over the edge of the top dough. With your fingers or a fork, pinch the edges together firmly to seal. Brush the top with the remaining oil and pierce 3 or 4 times with a fork or knife. Bake for 15 to 18 minutes, or until lightly golden. Remove from the oven and spread the cheese over the top. Bake for 15 to 18 more minutes, or until the crust is crisp and brown. Let cool for 3 to 5 minutes before cutting and serving.

Sloppy Joe Stuffed Pizza

6 to 8 slices

Sloppy Joes are an American favorite, so if you've got any teenagers at your house, you're sure to have all the neighborhood kids knocking at your door when they find out you're making them on pizza!

Pizza dough of your choice:

2 BATCHES HOMEMADE DOUGH   OR   **2 BATCHES STORE-BOUGHT DOUGH**

Prepare 2 batches Traditional Pizza Dough (page 3), steps 1 through 4. Make pizza as directed below.

Prepare 2 batches dough (pages 10–12), steps 1 and 2. Make pizza as directed below.

1 pound ground beef
1/2 cup spaghetti sauce
1/2 cup salsa
1 teaspoon salt
1 tablespoon olive oil

1/2 cup (2 ounces) shredded Cheddar cheese
1/2 cup (2 ounces) shredded mozzarella cheese

Preheat the oven to 400°F. In a large skillet, brown the ground beef over medium heat for 8 to 10 minutes, or until no pink remains. Drain off the excess liquid and add the spaghetti sauce, salsa, and salt; mix well. Spread the mixture evenly onto one of the rounds of dough, leaving a 1-inch border all around. Remove the second dough from the pizza pan and place it over the meat mixture. Bring the edge of the bottom dough up over the edge of the top dough. With your fingers or a fork, pinch the edges together firmly to seal. Brush the top with the oil and pierce 3 or 4 times with a fork or knife. Bake for 15 to 17 minutes, or until golden. Remove the pizza from the oven. In a small bowl, combine the 2 cheeses. Sprinkle the cheeses over the top of the pizza and bake for 10 more minutes, or until the crust is crisp and brown. Cut and serve.

NOTE: For true homemade taste, substitute 1 cup Spicy Chunky Pizza Sauce (page 15) for the spaghetti sauce and salsa.

Stuffed Eggplant Pizza

6 to 8 slices

Eggplant sure goes a long way. And as reasonably priced as it is, why not make this inexpensive stuffed pizza? They'll love the taste so much, they won't even realize how nutritious it is.

Pizza dough of your choice:

2 BATCHES HOMEMADE DOUGH OR **2 BATCHES STORE-BOUGHT DOUGH**

Prepare 2 batches Traditional Pizza Dough (page 3), steps 1 through 4. Make pizza as directed below.

Prepare 2 batches dough (pages 10–12), steps 1 and 2. Make pizza as directed below.

1/3 cup plus 1 tablespoon olive oil, divided
4 garlic cloves, minced
2 medium-sized eggplants, peeled and cubed (about 8 cups)

1 large onion, chopped (about 1 1/4 cups)
1 1/4 cups pizza or spaghetti sauce
2 teaspoons salt
1/2 teaspoon pepper

Preheat the oven to 400°F. In a large skillet, heat 1/3 cup of the olive oil over medium heat. Add the garlic and sauté for about 1 minute. Add the eggplant and onion and sauté for 15 to 17 minutes, until the eggplant is tender. Add the sauce, salt, and pepper; stir until well mixed. Spread the mixture evenly onto one of the rounds of dough, leaving a 1-inch border all around. Remove the second dough from the pizza pan and place it over the eggplant mixture. Bring the edge of the bottom dough up over the edge of the top dough. With your fingers or a fork, pinch the edges together firmly to seal. Brush the top with the remaining 1 tablespoon oil and pierce 3 or 4 times with a fork or knife. Bake for 25 to 30 minutes or until the crust is crisp and brown. Cut and serve.

NOTE: No pizza or spaghetti sauce on hand? No problem. Simply whip up a batch of "No Time" Homemade Pizza Sauce (page 16).

Stuffed Turkey and Cranberry Pizza

6 to 8 slices

Thanksgiving on a pizza?! Yup, that's just what this is, and it sure is holiday-delicious.

Pizza dough of your choice:

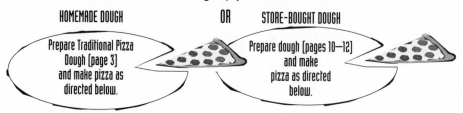

HOMEMADE DOUGH	OR	STORE-BOUGHT DOUGH
Prepare Traditional Pizza Dough [page 3] and make pizza as directed below.		Prepare dough [pages 10–12] and make pizza as directed below.

1 cup (about ⅔ of a 16-ounce can) whole-berry cranberry sauce

½ pound sliced deli turkey, coarsely chopped, or 2 cups coarsely chopped leftover cooked turkey

4 servings one-step stuffing, prepared according to the package directions and kept warm

Preheat the oven to 450°F. Bake the dough for 7 to 9 minutes, just until golden. Remove from the oven and let cool. Spread the cranberry sauce evenly over the prepared crust, then top with the turkey. Cover the turkey and cranberry sauce completely with the warm stuffing, pressing down lightly. Bake for 8 to 10 minutes, or until the crust is crisp and brown. Cut and serve.

NOTE: If you've got it, you can use 2 cups of your own leftover homemade stuffing.

Shepherd's Pie Pizza

6 to 8 slices

The English are famous for this classic dish. Now, with a slight twist, it's an all-in-one pizza recipe that not only makes dinner a pleasure, it also cleans up in a snap.

Pizza dough of your choice:

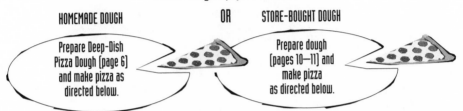

HOMEMADE DOUGH OR **STORE-BOUGHT DOUGH**

Prepare Deep-Dish Pizza Dough [page 6] and make pizza as directed below.

Prepare dough [pages 10—11] and make pizza as directed below.

1 pound ground beef
2 envelopes (from a 2-ounce box) onion soup mix
1 package (10 ounces) frozen mixed vegetables, thawed and drained
4 servings warm instant mashed potatoes, prepared according to the package directions

1/2 teaspoon dried sage
1/2 teaspoon garlic powder
1 egg
3/4 cup (3 ounces) shredded Cheddar cheese

Preheat the oven to 350°F. Bake the dough for 7 to 9 minutes, just until golden. Remove from the oven and set aside. In a large skillet, brown the ground beef over medium-low heat for 10 to 12 minutes or until no pink remains; drain off the excess liquid. Add the soup mix and stir well. Add the vegetables; remove from the heat and set aside. Place the mashed potatoes in a medium-sized bowl and add the sage, garlic powder, egg, and cheese; mix well. Spread the meat mixture evenly over the prepared crust, then spread the potatoes carefully over the top. Bake for 40 to 45 minutes, or until the potato topping begins to brown and the crust is golden. Cut and serve.

Southern Stuffed Corn Pizza

6 to 8 slices

This pizza is so simple you'll think that you made a mistake! But when you taste this combination, you'll know that you made something that's almost perfect!

HOMEMADE DOUGH

Prepare Cornmeal Dough [page 5], steps 1 through 3. Make pizza as directed below.

2 teaspoons olive oil, divided

2 cups (8 ounces) shredded Monterey Jack cheese

Preheat the oven to 450°F. Divide the dough into 2 balls. Place each ball on a 12-inch pizza pan that has been coated with nonstick vegetable spray, and spread each dough ball with your fingertips or the heel of your hand to make a 12-inch circle. Brush each circle with 1 teaspoon oil. Bake for 7 to 9 minutes, just until golden. Remove from the oven and sprinkle the cheese over 1 crust. Place the other crust, top side down, over the cheese. Bake for 5 more minutes, or until the cheese melts and the crust is crisp and brown. Cut and serve.

NOTE: If you don't have two 12-inch pizza pans, bake one dough circle at a time, then assemble the pizza and bake.

Puffed Pesto Chicken Pizza

6 to 8 servings

This pizza has a nice, light difference...it's got a puff pastry crust for a change.

2 frozen puff pastry sheets
(from a 17.25-ounce package), thawed
1 tablespoon olive oil
6 boneless, skinless chicken breast halves
(about 1½ pounds), cut into ¼-inch cubes
¼ teaspoon salt
½ cup Homemade Pesto Sauce
(page 18) or prepared pesto
½ cup White Pizza Sauce (page 17)

Preheat the oven to 400°F. On a lightly floured surface, roll out each puff pastry sheet to a rectangle about 10" × 14"; set aside. In a large skillet, heat the oil over medium heat. Add the chicken, sprinkle with the salt, and sauté for 4 to 5 minutes, or until no pink remains. Remove from the heat and drain off the excess liquid. Add the sauces and stir until the chicken is well coated. Spread half of the mixture lengthwise down the center of each pastry sheet, then fold in half lengthwise. With your fingers or a fork, pinch the edges together to seal. Place seam side down on a rimmed cookie sheet and bake for 20 to 25 minutes, or until the pastry is golden brown. Cut and serve.

Spinach and Ricotta Calzones

4 calzones

I first had a spinach-stuffed calzone in New York City's Little Italy, and this is my version to share with you. Maybe for dessert you can go for an Italian ice, like I did.

Pizza dough of your choice:

2 BATCHES HOMEMADE DOUGH   **OR**   **2 BATCHES STORE-BOUGHT DOUGH**

Prepare 2 batches Traditional Pizza Dough [page 3], steps 1 through 3. Make calzones as directed below.

Prepare 2 batches dough [pages 10–12], step 1 only. Make calzones as directed below.

1 container (15 ounces) ricotta cheese
5 ounces ($\frac{1}{2}$ a 10-ounce box) frozen chopped spinach, thawed and well drained
1 teaspoon onion powder
1 teaspoon garlic powder

1 tablespoon Italian seasoning
$\frac{1}{8}$ teaspoon ground nutmeg
$1\frac{1}{2}$ teaspoons salt
$\frac{1}{4}$ teaspoon pepper
1 tablespoon plus 1 teaspoon olive oil

Preheat the oven to 450°F. In a medium-sized bowl, combine all of the filling ingredients except the oil and mix until well blended; set aside. Divide each batch of dough into 2 balls. On a lightly floured surface, spread each dough ball with your fingertips or the heel of your hand to make a 7- to 8-inch circle. Spread one quarter of the spinach mixture on each dough circle, forming a semicircle of filling on half of each dough and leaving a $\frac{1}{2}$-inch border around the edge (see diagram page 117). Fold the dough over the filling, forming half-moons. With your fingers or a fork, pinch the edges together firmly to seal. Place the calzones on 2 cookie sheets that have been coated with nonstick vegetable spray and brush the top of each with 1 teaspoon oil. Pierce the tops 3 or 4 times with a fork or knife. Bake for 15 to 18 minutes, or until the crust is golden brown. Serve whole or cut as desired (page xxv).

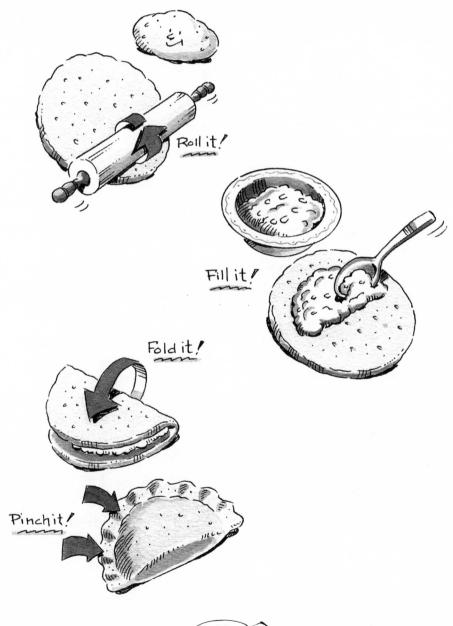

Italian Sausage and Mushroom Calzones

2 calzones

Now, *this* is Italian! When you taste this you'll think you're in a little village in southern Italy. It's almost as good as being there.

Pizza dough of your choice:

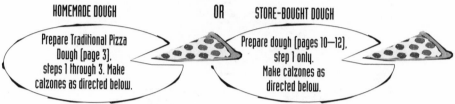

HOMEMADE DOUGH	OR	STORE-BOUGHT DOUGH
Prepare Traditional Pizza Dough (page 3), steps 1 through 3. Make calzones as directed below.		Prepare dough (pages 10–12), step 1 only. Make calzones as directed below.

8 ounces hot or sweet Italian sausage, casings removed
1 can (4 ounces) mushroom stems and pieces, drained
1/4 cup pizza or spaghetti sauce

1 teaspoon Italian seasoning
1/2 cup (2 ounces) shredded mozzarella cheese, divided
2 teaspoons olive oil, divided

Preheat the oven to 450°F. In a medium-sized nonstick skillet, brown the sausage over medium heat for 6 to 8 minutes, stirring occasionally. Add the mushrooms and sauté for 2 minutes, until no pink remains in the sausage. Remove from the heat and drain off the excess liquid. Stir in the sauce and Italian seasoning; set aside. Divide the dough into 2 balls. On a lightly floured surface, spread each dough ball with your fingertips or the heel of your hand to make a 7- to 8-inch circle. Spread half of the sausage mixture onto each dough circle, forming a semicircle of filling on half of each dough and leaving a 1/2-inch border around the edge (see diagram page 117). Top each with 1/4 cup mozzarella cheese. Fold the dough over the filling, forming half-moons. With your fingers or a fork, pinch the edges together firmly to seal. Place the calzones on a cookie sheet that has been coated with nonstick vegetable spray and brush the top of each with 1 teaspoon oil. Pierce the tops 3 or 4 times with a fork or knife. Bake for 18 to 22 minutes, or until the crust is golden brown. Serve whole or cut as desired (page xxv).

Portobello and Jack Calzones

2 calzones

Portobello mushrooms are so versatile that you can use them in almost any dish. But they're so delicious in this calzone, you'll think it's what they were made for.

Pizza dough of your choice:

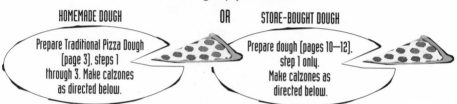

HOMEMADE DOUGH

Prepare Traditional Pizza Dough (page 3), steps 1 through 3. Make calzones as directed below.

OR

STORE-BOUGHT DOUGH

Prepare dough (pages 10–12), step 1 only. Make calzones as directed below.

2 tablespoons olive oil, divided
3 garlic cloves, minced
8 ounces Portobello mushrooms, cut into ¾-inch slices
¼ teaspoon salt

⅛ teaspoon pepper
½ cup (2 ounces) shredded Monterey Jack cheese, divided

Preheat the oven to 425°F. In a large skillet, heat 1 tablespoon of the oil over medium-high heat. Add the garlic and sauté for 1 minute. Add the mushrooms, salt, and pepper and sauté for 3 to 5 minutes, or until the mushrooms are tender. Remove from the heat. Divide the dough into 2 balls. On a lightly floured surface, spread each dough ball with your fingertips or the heel of your hand to make a 7- to 8-inch circle. Spoon half of the mushroom mixture onto each dough circle, forming a semicircle of filling on half of each dough and leaving a ½-inch border around the edge (see diagram page 117). Top each with ¼ cup cheese. Fold the dough over the filling, forming half-moons. With your fingers or a fork, pinch the edges together firmly to seal. Place the calzones on a cookie sheet that has been coated with nonstick vegetable spray and brush the tops with the remaining 1 tablespoon of oil. Pierce the tops 3 or 4 times with a fork or knife. Bake for 16 to 18 minutes, or until the crust is golden brown. Serve whole or cut as desired (page xxv).

Ham and Swiss Calzones

2 calzones

Ham and Swiss has always been one of my favorite combinations, whether in sandwiches, salads, or whatever. Now that I've teamed them in calzones, they're still a favorite...and I'll bet they'll be a hit with you, too.

Pizza dough of your choice:

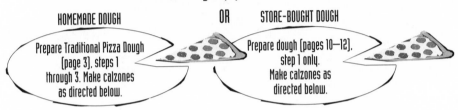

HOMEMADE DOUGH   **OR**   **STORE-BOUGHT DOUGH**

Prepare Traditional Pizza Dough [page 3], steps 1 through 3. Make calzones as directed below.

Prepare dough [pages 10–12], step 1 only. Make calzones as directed below.

2 cans (5 ounces each) chunked ham, drained and flaked
2 cups (8 ounces) shredded Swiss cheese

2 teaspoons olive oil, divided

Preheat the oven to 450°F. In a medium-sized bowl, combine the ham and cheese; mix well and set aside. Divide the dough into 2 balls. Spread each dough ball with your fingertips or the heel of your hand to make a 7- to 8-inch circle. Spoon half of the ham mixture onto the center of each dough circle, forming a semicircle of filling on half of each dough and leaving a 1/2-inch border around the edge (see diagram page 117). Fold the dough over the filling, forming half-moons. With your fingers or a fork, pinch the edges together firmly to seal. Place the calzones on a cookie sheet that has been coated with nonstick vegetable spray and brush the top of each with 1 teaspoon oil. Pierce the tops 3 or 4 times with a fork or knife. Bake for 15 to 17 minutes, or until the crust is golden brown. Serve whole or cut as desired (page xxv).

Four-Cheese Calzones

2 calzones

Cheese, cheese, cheese, cheese! I love it so much I can never get enough! One of these calzones comes close to satisfying my appetite for cheese, but I always cook both, just in case.

Pizza dough of your choice:

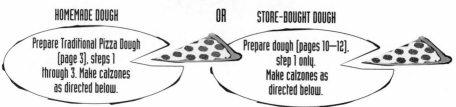

HOMEMADE DOUGH

Prepare Traditional Pizza Dough (page 3), steps 1 through 3. Make calzones as directed below.

OR

STORE-BOUGHT DOUGH

Prepare dough (pages 10–12), step 1 only. Make calzones as directed below.

¹/₄ cup ricotta cheese
2 tablespoons grated Parmesan cheese
2 tablespoons crumbled Gorgonzola cheese
¹/₄ cup shredded mozzarella cheese

1 egg
¹/₄ teaspoon dried basil
¹/₈ teaspoon pepper
¹/₄ cup chopped fresh parsley
2 teaspoons olive oil, divided

Preheat the oven to 450°F. In a small bowl, combine all of the filling ingredients except the oil. Mix until well blended; set aside. Divide each batch of dough into 2 balls. On a lightly floured surface, spread each dough ball with your fingertips or the heel of your hand to make a 7- to 8-inch circle. Spoon half of the cheese mixture onto each dough circle, forming a semicircle of filling on half of each and leaving a ¹/₂-inch border around the edge (see diagram page 117). Fold the dough over the filling, forming half-moons. With your fingers or a fork, pinch the edges together firmly to seal. Place the calzones on a cookie sheet that has been coated with nonstick vegetable spray and brush the top of each with 1 teaspoon oil. Pierce the tops 3 or 4 times with a fork or knife. Bake for 12 to 14 minutes, or until the crust is golden brown. Serve whole or cut and serve as desired (page xxv).

Tuna and Spinach Calzones

4 calzones

Make these ahead of time and refrigerate them. Then you've got your lunch or dinner by simply popping them in a 300°F. oven for 15 minutes!

Pizza dough of your choice:

2 BATCHES HOMEMADE DOUGH

Prepare 2 batches Traditional Pizza Dough (page 3), steps 1 through 3. Make calzones as directed below.

OR 2 BATCHES STORE-BOUGHT DOUGH

Prepare 2 batches dough (pages 10–12), step 1 only. Make calzones as directed below.

2 cans (6 ounces each) water-packed tuna, well drained and flaked
1/2 cup mayonnaise
1 small onion, chopped (about 1/2 cup)
1/2 cup slivered almonds
1 cup (4 ounces) shredded Swiss cheese

1 package (10 ounces) frozen chopped spinach, thawed and well drained
1/8 teaspoon ground nutmeg
1/4 teaspoon garlic powder
1/2 teaspoon salt
1/4 teaspoon pepper
1 tablespoon plus 1 teaspoon olive oil, divided

Preheat the oven to 450°F. In a large bowl, combine the tuna and mayonnaise and mix until well blended. Add the remaining filling ingredients except the oil; mix well and set aside. Divide each batch of dough into 2 balls. On a lightly floured surface, spread each dough ball with your fingertips or the heel of your hand to make a 7- to 8-inch circle. Spread one quarter of the tuna mixture onto the center of each dough circle, forming a semicircle of filling on half of each dough and leaving a 1/2-inch border around the edge (see diagram page 117). Fold the dough over the filling, forming half-moons. With your fingers or a fork, pinch the edges together firmly to seal. Place the calzones on 2 cookie sheets that have been coated with nonstick vegetable spray and brush the top of each with 1 teaspoon oil. Pierce the tops 3 or 4 times with a fork or knife. Bake for 18 to 22 minutes, or until the crust is golden brown. Serve whole or cut as desired (page xxv).

Pizzas That Think They're Sandwiches

Okay, so these aren't traditional pizzas either. They're pizzas with an identity crisis! I mean they're pizzas that have the tastes and textures of some of my (and everyone's) favorite sandwiches.

I'm not trying to confuse your taste buds but, after all, pizza crust *is* kind of like bread. So now that we've cleared that up, you've got to do me (and yourself) a favor and try my B.L.T. Pizza (page 129), Reuben Pizza (page 135), and the others. You'll be pleasantly surprised.

And please promise that the next time you can't decide between a pizza or a sandwich you'll compromise and have a pizza that tastes like a sandwich—it'll be twice as good! Delis around the world: Beware!

Pizzas That Think
They're Sandwiches

Italian Hoagie Pizza

6 to 8 slices

Talk about things that go together...how many times have you been in a pizzeria and seen not only pizza but a whole selection of submarine sandwiches on the menu, too? Well, I took the liberty of trying out submarine ingredients on a pizza. I bet the combo catches on!

Pizza base of your choice:

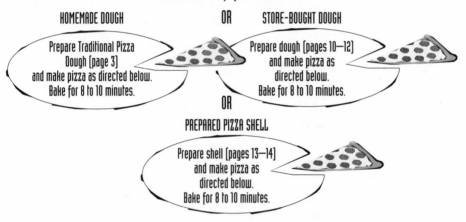

HOMEMADE DOUGH

Prepare Traditional Pizza Dough (page 3) and make pizza as directed below. Bake for 8 to 10 minutes.

OR

STORE-BOUGHT DOUGH

Prepare dough (pages 10–12) and make pizza as directed below. Bake for 8 to 10 minutes.

OR

PREPARED PIZZA SHELL

Prepare shell (pages 13–14) and make pizza as directed below. Bake for 8 to 10 minutes.

¼ pound sliced deli ham, cut into 1-inch pieces
¼ pound sliced deli salami, cut into 1-inch pieces
1 cup chopped plum tomatoes (2 to 3 tomatoes)

¼ cup Italian dressing
One package (6 ounces) sliced provolone cheese
1 teaspoon Italian seasoning

Preheat the oven to 450°F. If using Traditional Pizza Dough or store-bought dough, bake for 7 to 9 minutes, just until golden. Remove from the oven and set aside. In a medium-sized bowl, combine the ham, salami, tomatoes, and dressing; mix well. Spoon the mixture evenly over the prepared crust and top with the cheese. Sprinkle with the Italian seasoning and bake as directed above, or until the crust is crisp and brown. Cut and serve.

B.L.T. Pizza

6 to 8 slices

Here's an anytime, anywhere pizza that tastes just like its namesake sandwich. Go ahead and serve it with pickle chips on the side.

Pizza base of your choice:

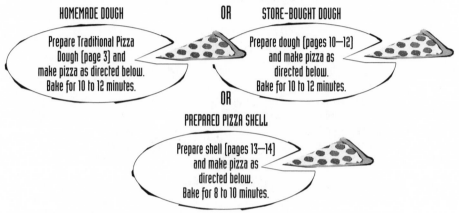

HOMEMADE DOUGH

Prepare Traditional Pizza Dough [page 3] and make pizza as directed below. Bake for 10 to 12 minutes.

OR

STORE-BOUGHT DOUGH

Prepare dough [pages 10–12] and make pizza as directed below. Bake for 10 to 12 minutes.

OR

PREPARED PIZZA SHELL

Prepare shell [pages 13–14] and make pizza as directed below. Bake for 8 to 10 minutes.

1 pound bacon cooked until crisp, drained, and crumbled (about 1 cup)
1 medium-sized tomato, chopped and drained (about 1¼ cups)

2 cups chopped iceberg lettuce
¼ cup mayonnaise

Preheat the oven to 450°F. Spread the cooked bacon evenly over the prepared base, then top with the tomato. Bake as directed above, or until the crust is crisp and brown. Meanwhile, in a medium-sized bowl, combine the lettuce and mayonnaise; toss until the lettuce is well coated. Top the pizza with the lettuce mixture; cut and serve immediately.

Cheeseburger Pizza

6 to 8 slices

You've been there...driving down the main drag with the whole gang in the back trying to decide where to eat. "I want pizza!" "I want a burger!" Maybe next time you'll surprise them by driving home and making something that everybody will agree on. Give this a try!

Pizza base of your choice:

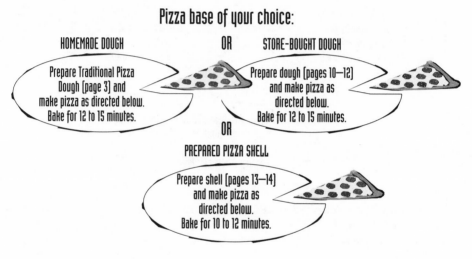

HOMEMADE DOUGH

Prepare Traditional Pizza Dough (page 3) and make pizza as directed below. Bake for 12 to 15 minutes.

OR

STORE-BOUGHT DOUGH

Prepare dough (pages 10–12) and make pizza as directed below. Bake for 12 to 15 minutes.

OR

PREPARED PIZZA SHELL

Prepare shell (pages 13–14) and make pizza as directed below. Bake for 10 to 12 minutes.

½ pound ground beef
1 small onion, chopped
   (about ½ cup)
2 teaspoons chopped garlic
   (2 cloves)
½ cup ketchup
½ teaspoon prepared yellow
   mustard

¼ teaspoon salt
¼ teaspoon pepper
¼ cup coarsely chopped dill
   pickles
1 cup (4 ounces) shredded
   Cheddar cheese

In a medium-sized skillet, brown the ground beef over medium-high heat for 4 to 5 minutes, or until no pink remains. Remove from the heat and drain off the excess liquid. Return the skillet to the heat and add the onion and garlic. Sauté for 2 minutes, or just until the onion is tender. Add the ketchup, mustard, salt, and pepper; mix well. Spread the beef mixture evenly over the prepared base. Sprinkle with the pickles and top with the cheese. Bake as directed above, or until the crust is crisp and brown. Cut and serve.

Crunchy Tuna Melt Pizza

6 to 8 slices

When I was growing up, I'd go to my favorite diner to order a tuna melt and a chocolate milk shake. Well, the diner isn't around anymore, but I can enjoy the memories when I make this pizza. Hey! Don't forget the chocolate shake!

Pizza base of your choice:

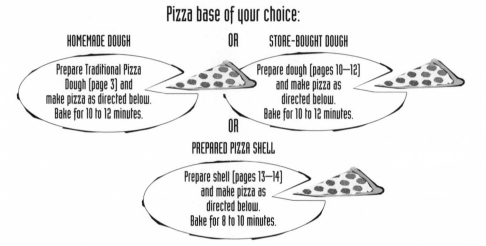

HOMEMADE DOUGH OR **STORE-BOUGHT DOUGH**

Prepare Traditional Pizza Dough (page 3) and make pizza as directed below. Bake for 10 to 12 minutes.

Prepare dough (pages 10–12) and make pizza as directed below. Bake for 10 to 12 minutes.

OR

PREPARED PIZZA SHELL

Prepare shell (pages 13–14) and make pizza as directed below. Bake for 8 to 10 minutes.

2 cans (6 ounces each) water-packed tuna, well drained and flaked
1/2 cup mayonnaise

1 cup (4 ounces) shredded Havarti cheese
3/4 cup coarsely crushed potato chips

Preheat the oven to 450°F. In a small bowl, combine the tuna and mayonnaise and mix until well blended. Spread evenly over the prepared base and top with the Havarti cheese. Sprinkle with the crushed chips and bake as directed above, or until the crust is crisp and brown. Cut and serve.

State Fair Pizza

6 to 8 slices

I go to the fair for the popcorn, cotton candy, and three rides for a dollar. Oh, and of course for those famous sausage sandwiches that keep me going back year after year!

Pizza base of your choice:

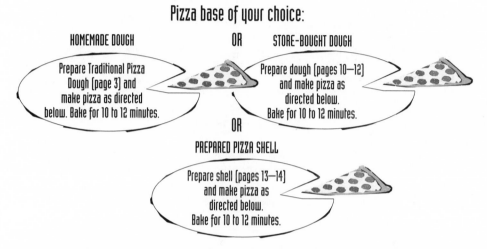

HOMEMADE DOUGH   OR   **STORE-BOUGHT DOUGH**

Prepare Traditional Pizza Dough [page 3] and make pizza as directed below. Bake for 10 to 12 minutes.

Prepare dough [pages 10–12] and make pizza as directed below. Bake for 10 to 12 minutes.

OR

PREPARED PIZZA SHELL

Prepare shell [pages 13–14] and make pizza as directed below. Bake for 10 to 12 minutes.

½ pound hot Italian sausage, cut into ½-inch slices
½ a medium-sized green bell pepper, cut into ¼-inch strips
½ a medium-sized red bell pepper, cut into ¼-inch strips
1 small onion, halved and cut into ¼-inch strips
⅓ cup pizza or spaghetti sauce

Preheat the oven to 450°F. If using Traditional Pizza Dough or store-bought dough, bake for 7 to 9 minutes, just until golden. Remove from the oven and set aside. In a large skillet, cook the sausage over medium heat, stirring occasionally, for 4 to 6 minutes, or until lightly browned. Reduce the heat to low, add the bell peppers and onion, and cook for 10 to 15 minutes, until the onions are browned and the peppers are very tender, stirring occasionally. Remove from the heat and drain off the excess liquid. Spread the sauce over the prepared crust and top with the sausage mixture. Bake as directed above, or until the crust is crisp and brown. Cut and serve.

Turkey Club Pizza

6 to 8 slices

There are social clubs and business clubs, and now I've got a "club" that *everybody* wants to be part of!

Pizza base of your choice:

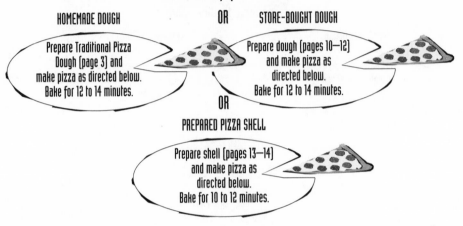

HOMEMADE DOUGH

Prepare Traditional Pizza Dough (page 3) and make pizza as directed below. Bake for 12 to 14 minutes.

OR

STORE-BOUGHT DOUGH

Prepare dough (pages 10–12) and make pizza as directed below. Bake for 12 to 14 minutes.

OR

PREPARED PIZZA SHELL

Prepare shell (pages 13–14) and make pizza as directed below. Bake for 10 to 12 minutes.

1 cup (4 ounces) shredded Cheddar cheese
½ pound sliced deli turkey breast, cut into 1-inch pieces
¼ cup bacon bits

2 cups shredded iceberg lettuce
1 medium-sized tomato, chopped (about 1¼ cups)

Preheat the oven to 450°F. Spread the cheese evenly over the prepared base, then top with the turkey. Sprinkle with the bacon bits and bake as directed above, or until the crust is crisp and brown. Top with the shredded lettuce and chopped tomatoes; cut and serve.

Reuben Pizza

6 to 8 slices

I love the taste of Reuben sandwiches, but they sure are messy to eat. I think I've found a trick for enjoying that same great deli taste *without* having to use so many napkins.

Pizza base of your choice:

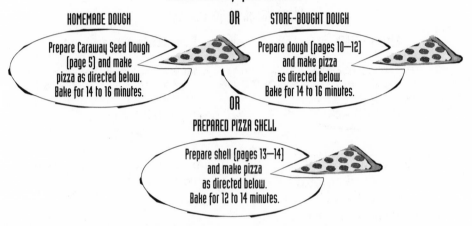

HOMEMADE DOUGH

Prepare Caraway Seed Dough (page 5) and make pizza as directed below. Bake for 14 to 16 minutes.

OR

STORE-BOUGHT DOUGH

Prepare dough (pages 10–12) and make pizza as directed below. Bake for 14 to 16 minutes.

OR

PREPARED PIZZA SHELL

Prepare shell (pages 13–14) and make pizza as directed below. Bake for 12 to 14 minutes.

1 can (14.4 ounces) sauerkraut, drained and squeezed dry
6 ounces sliced corned beef, cut into 1/2-inch strips

1/2 cup Russian dressing
1 cup (4 ounces) shredded Swiss cheese

Preheat the oven to 450°F. Sprinkle the sauerkraut over the prepared base and set aside. In a small bowl, combine the corned beef and dressing; toss to coat. Spoon over the sauerkraut and top with the Swiss cheese. Bake as directed above, or until the crust is crisp and brown. Cut and serve.

Philly Cheese Steak Pizza

6 to 8 slices

I travel to Philadelphia quite a bit during the year, so I know about all the super people there *and* the super Philly cheese steak sandwiches. I figured I would put that famous big Philly taste on a pizza shell. It's kind of like visiting Philadelphia's Little Italy.

Pizza dough of your choice:

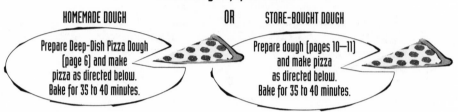

HOMEMADE DOUGH

Prepare Deep-Dish Pizza Dough (page 6) and make pizza as directed below. Bake for 35 to 40 minutes.

OR

STORE-BOUGHT DOUGH

Prepare dough (pages 10–11) and make pizza as directed below. Bake for 35 to 40 minutes.

2 tablespoons olive oil
2 medium-sized onions, halved and sliced ¼ inch thick
1 pound sliced deli roast beef, cut into ½-inch strips

1 cup (4 ounces) shredded Swiss cheese

Preheat the oven to 400°F. Bake the dough for 7 to 9 minutes, just until golden. Remove from the oven and set aside. In a large skillet, heat the oil over medium-high heat and sauté the onions for 12 to 14 minutes, or until soft and golden. Remove from the heat and stir in the roast beef. Spoon the mixture onto the prepared crust and top with the cheese. Bake as directed above, or until the crust is crisp and brown. Cut and serve.

Lox, Cream Cheese, and Onion Pizza

6 to 8 slices

Oh, boy! You're gonna love this one! When I tried this in my test kitchen, it disappeared before I got a chance to try it! Everybody wanted the last piece, and so will you…time after time.

Pizza base of your choice:

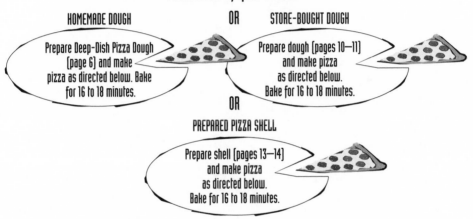

HOMEMADE DOUGH

Prepare Deep-Dish Pizza Dough [page 6] and make pizza as directed below. Bake for 16 to 18 minutes.

OR

STORE-BOUGHT DOUGH

Prepare dough [pages 10–11] and make pizza as directed below. Bake for 16 to 18 minutes.

OR

PREPARED PIZZA SHELL

Prepare shell [pages 13–14] and make pizza as directed below. Bake for 16 to 18 minutes.

1 package (8 ounces) cream cheese, softened
1/2 a small onion, finely chopped (about 1/4 cup)
2 tablespoons chopped fresh chives or 2 teaspoons dried chives

3 medium-sized plum tomatoes, seeded and coarsely chopped (about 1 cup)
2 ounces smoked salmon, chopped
1/4 teaspoon pepper

Preheat the oven to 400°F. If using Deep-Dish Pizza Dough or store-bought dough, bake for 12 to 14 minutes, just until golden. Remove from the oven and set aside. In a small bowl, combine the cream cheese, onion, and chives and mix until well blended. Spread the cream cheese mixture evenly over the prepared crust, leaving a ¹/₂-inch border all around. Top with the tomatoes and salmon, then sprinkle with the pepper. Bake as directed above, or until the crust is crisp and brown. Cut and serve.

NOTE: For all those great Sunday-morning tastes in one, add 1 tablespoon poppy seeds to the Deep-Dish Pizza Dough.

Presto Pizzas

You know those times when you get home from work late, you've got nothing prepared for dinner, and you're famished? Or the kids get home from school and need something good and quick to tide them over till dinner? Or you've got the late-night munchies and have to have something *NOW*?!

Well, stop here! French Bread Pizza (page 143) and my other Presto Pizzas can all be ready in under 10 minutes. Sure, it's possible! Now, don't think the other pizzas in the book aren't quick and easy, 'cause they are—but these are *extra-quick* and *extra-easy* to get you through those frantic moments. And since these pizzas *are* so quick and easy, they're perfect for when the kids want to help. They'll especially like making the Happy Face Muffins (page 148). Why, they're sure to put a smile on *your* face, too!

Presto Pizzas

Pita Pizza

These little pizzas are great for a quick meal with friends. You'll be finished in the kitchen so fast that you'll have *lots* of time to visit!

Four 6-inch pita breads
$1/2$ cup pizza or spaghetti sauce
1 cup (4 ounces) shredded mozzarella cheese
$1/2$ teaspoon Italian seasoning
1 can (2.25 ounces) sliced black olives, drained ($1/2$ cup)
1 can (4 ounces) sliced mushrooms, drained
1 can (4 ounces) pimientos, drained and coarsely chopped

Preheat the oven to 450°F. Lay the pitas golden side down on a cookie sheet that has been coated with nonstick vegetable spray. Spread 2 tablespoons sauce evenly over each pita, then top each with $1/4$ cup cheese. Sprinkle $1/8$ teaspoon Italian seasoning over each pita, then top with the remaining ingredients, dividing them evenly. Bake for 12 to 15 minutes, or until the cheese begins to brown and bubble. Serve whole or cut as desired.

French Bread Pizza

10 to 12 slices

French bread is one of my favorites, and I love it even more as a pizza "crust" with just a few great toppings. See for yourself!

1 loaf (1 pound) French bread
1 1/4 cups pizza or spaghetti sauce
1 1/4 cups (5 ounces) shredded mozzarella cheese
1 teaspoon Italian seasoning
1/4 cup grated Parmesan cheese

Preheat the broiler. Cut the French bread in half lengthwise and place it cut side up on a cookie sheet. Broil for 2 to 3 minutes, or until lightly browned. Remove from the broiler and spread half the sauce evenly over each half, followed by the mozzarella cheese. Sprinkle with the Italian seasoning and top with the Parmesan cheese. Broil for 1 to 2 minutes, then rotate the pan and broil for 2 to 3 more minutes, or until the cheeses are lightly browned and bubbly. Cut and serve.

NOTE: Hey, just because I like these toppings doesn't mean that you can't use different ones. Check out my topping list (page 25) or add your own favorites.

"Everything" Bagelettes

20 mini-pizzas

You know what these are perfect for? Everything! They make a great party appetizer or a quick dinner for a group of hungry kids. Either way, you'll be a kitchen hero.

1 package (9 ounces) frozen mini-bagels,
thawed and split in half
1 cup (4 ounces) shredded mozzarella cheese
$1/2$ cup grated Parmesan cheese
1 can (6 ounces) tomato paste
$1/2$ teaspoon garlic powder
$1/4$ teaspoon dried oregano
$1/4$ teaspoon dried basil
$1/2$ teaspoon salt
$1/8$ teaspoon pepper

Preheat the broiler. Place the bagel halves cut side up on a cookie sheet that has been coated with nonstick vegetable spray. In a large bowl, combine the remaining ingredients. Spread evenly over the bagel halves. Broil for 7 to 9 minutes, or until the bagels are crisp and the cheese has melted. Serve.

NOTE: Sprinkle with chopped fresh parsley if you'd like.

Bacon 'n' Cheddar Bagel Classic

12 bagel pizzas

Bacon and Cheddar cheese is a classic combination—one that's popular even at fast-food restaurants. It doesn't get any easier than this, and once you make these, I know you'll agree!

6 bagels, thawed if frozen, split in half
1^1/$_3$ cups pizza or spaghetti sauce
^{1}/$_2$ cup bacon bits
1 cup (4 ounces) shredded Cheddar cheese

Preheat the oven to 350°F. Place the bagel halves cut side up on a cookie sheet. Spoon the sauce evenly over the bagel halves, sprinkle with the bacon bits, and top with the cheese. Bake for 12 to 15 minutes, or until the bagels are crisp and the cheese has melted. Serve.

Spicy Salsa Muffin Pizzas

12 muffin pizzas

You want quick, right? You want easy, too? Well, how 'bout spicy? These great little pizzas have it all. (You won't be able to stop eating them!)

6 English muffins, split in half
1 jar (8 ounces) salsa
2 tablespoons bottled chopped jalapeño peppers, drained
1 cup (4 ounces) shredded Cheddar cheese

Preheat the oven to 450°F. Place the muffin halves cut side up on a cookie sheet. Spoon the salsa evenly over them, then top with the jalapeños and cheese. Bake for 7 to 9 minutes, or until the muffins are crisp and the cheese begins to brown. Serve.

NOTE: If you like a crisp muffin, bake the muffins first for 4 to 6 minutes, then top and bake for 6 to 8 minutes. I like to split the muffins using the tines of a fork; the sauce and toppings seem to stay on better that way.

Tortilla Pizza Roll-ups

10 roll-ups

This is a little pizza combination that's really different—and fun, too! Your kids will want to help with these, 'cause they're as much fun to make as they are to eat!

Ten 7-inch flour tortillas
1 cup pizza or spaghetti sauce
1 medium-sized green bell pepper, chopped (about 1 cup)
1 medium-sized onion, chopped (about 1 cup)
2 cups (8 ounces) shredded mozzarella cheese

Preheat the oven to 450°F. Place the tortillas on a clean work surface and spoon the sauce evenly over them. Sprinkle equal amounts of pepper, onion, and cheese over each one. Roll up the tortillas and place seam side down in a 9" × 13" baking dish that has been coated with nonstick vegetable spray. Bake for 12 to 15 minutes, or until the cheese is melted. Serve immediately.

NOTE: A little extra warm sauce is perfect for dipping these roll-ups. You can also assemble these up to 2 hours ahead of time (cover them and keep chilled). Then all you have to do is uncover and bake them before serving.

Happy Face Muffins

12 muffin pizzas

If you make these for your kids or grandkids, you'll know why we call them Happy Faces...'cause that's what you'll see across the table when you serve them!

6 English muffins, split in half
1 cup pizza or spaghetti sauce
1 package (6 ounces) sliced mozzarella cheese,
each slice cut into 2 circles (see Note)
6 slices pepperoni, cut in half
24 pitted black olives, sliced into rings
Four 1-inch ready-made frozen meatballs,
thawed and quartered

Preheat the oven to 450°F. Place the muffin halves cut side up on a cookie sheet. Spoon 1 tablespoon sauce over each muffin half and cover with a cheese circle. Place a pepperoni half on the bottom edge of each cheese circle to make a mouth. Place 2 olive slices near the top edge to make eyes. Place a meatball half in the center to make a nose. Bake for 7 to 9 minutes, or until the muffins are crisp and the cheese has melted. Allow to cool for a few minutes before serving.

NOTE: Use a 2³/4-inch cookie cutter or the rim of a round drinking glass to cut the cheese circles.

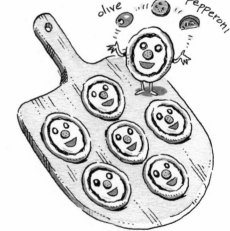

Mom's Cheese Melts

12 muffin pizzas

When I was growing up, I had these a lot, 'cause they were my mom's version of quick pizza. Boy, I loved them as a kid and, to tell you the truth, I like them just as well now!

6 English muffins, split in half
1/4 cup (1/2 stick) butter, softened
2 medium-sized tomatoes, each sliced
into six 1/4-inch slices
12 slices (9 ounces) American cheese

Preheat the broiler. Place the muffin halves cut side up on a cookie sheet. Spread the butter evenly over the muffin halves. Broil for 2 to 3 minutes, or until the edges begin to brown. Remove from the broiler. Place a tomato slice, then a cheese slice on each half. Broil for 2 to 3 minutes, or until the cheese begins to brown. Remove from the broiler and serve.

NOTE: Today there are so many sliced cheese choices that we're certainly not limited to American cheese. Why not use Cheddar slices one time, Muenster another, and on and on.

Herbed Pizza Rounds

8 rounds

Let me share a quick garlic pizza that works as a snack or a meal go-along.

1 large package (17.3 ounces)
refrigerated buttermilk biscuits (8 biscuits)
1/2 cup refrigerated herb and
garlic cheese spread
4 plum tomatoes, each sliced into 6 slices

Preheat the oven to 375°F. Separate the biscuits and flatten each with the palm of your hand to a circle about 3 1/2 inches across. Place on a cookie sheet that has been coated with nonstick vegetable spray and spread 1 tablespoon cheese spread on each biscuit. Top each with 3 tomato slices. Bake for 14 to 16 minutes, or until the biscuits are browned on the bottom. Serve.

NOTE: These are a must when you've got an abundance of summer garden-fresh plum tomatoes.

Surprise Pizza Puffs

8 puffs

When you bite into these, you'll get a surprise—delicious melted mozzarella cheese! After that you probably *won't* be surprised when you see how fast they disappear!

1 large package (17.3 ounces)
refrigerated biscuits (8 biscuits)
1/4 cup pizza or spaghetti sauce
2 ounces mozzarella cheese,
cut into eight 1-inch cubes

Preheat the oven to 450°F. Separate the biscuits and flatten each with the palm of your hand to a circle about 3½ inches across. Place on a cookie sheet that has been coated with nonstick vegetable spray. Spoon the pizza sauce evenly over the centers of the biscuits and place a mozzarella cube on each one. Pull the edges of each biscuit together so that the cheese is enclosed and pinch the edges firmly to seal. Turn the puffs over and bake for 8 to 10 minutes, or until golden brown. Serve warm.

NOTE: Be sure to buy a chunk of mozzarella cheese for this recipe, not sliced mozzarella.

Simple Italian Breads

If you want to drive your family wild with the smell of fresh-baked bread, try making some focaccia, bruschetta, or any of these other simple Italian breads. The smell alone is super, but the taste is big, too—I mean *really* big!

Oh, maybe I'd better explain what focaccia and bruschetta are. Focaccia is a flatbread that's usually rich in olive oil with an herb topping; it's kind of a cousin to pizza. In this chapter you'll find an Onion Focaccia (page 168) that'll satisfy any onion lover, not to mention a more traditional flavorful Herb Focaccia (page 166).

And bruschetta...that's toasted Italian bread flavored simply with olive oil and seasonings, or smothered in toppings of cheese, tomatoes, garlic, and olive oil. Watch out, it's addicting!

Then there's more! I've got easy recipes for homemade Bread Sticks (pages 169 and 170), traditional Italian Bread (page 161), and a selection of flavored butters and oils (pages 171 and 172)....Mmm!

So sit back with your big antipasto or bowl of minestrone soup and get ready to dunk a little, crunch a little, and hear lots of "ooh"s and "ahh"s before the big cheers of **"OOH IT'S SO GOOD!!**™**"**

Simple Italian Breads

Pizza Bread

1 loaf

This bread is so full of surprises that you won't know what to think when you bite into it. But don't worry, I promise you'll love it!

Pizza dough of your choice:

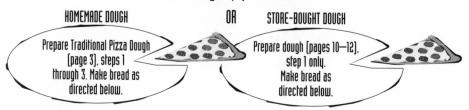

HOMEMADE DOUGH

Prepare Traditional Pizza Dough [page 3], steps 1 through 3. Make bread as directed below.

OR

STORE-BOUGHT DOUGH

Prepare dough [pages 10–12], step 1 only. Make bread as directed below.

1 teaspoon vegetable oil
¹/₄ cup finely chopped green bell pepper
¹/₂ a small onion, finely chopped (about ¹/₄ cup)

¹/₂ cup chopped pepperoni (2 to 3 ounces)
1 teaspoon Italian seasoning
³/₄ cup (3 ounces) shredded mozzarella cheese

Preheat the oven to 425°F. On a lightly floured surface, roll out the dough to a 9" × 15" rectangle. Brush with the oil, then sprinkle the pepper, onion, pepperoni, and Italian seasoning evenly over the dough. Sprinkle the cheese over the top. Roll up the dough jelly-roll fashion, starting at a 9-inch end. Tuck in the ends and place seam side down in a 5" × 9" loaf pan that has been coated with nonstick vegetable spray. Bake for 25 to 30 minutes, or until golden brown on top. Let cool slightly, then remove from the pan, slice, and serve.

NOTE: For best results, I suggest cutting this with a serrated knife.

Cheesy Corn Bread

1 loaf

Sometimes corn bread can seem, well, sort of bland. Not this one! With those sweet bell peppers and that delicious Monterey Jack cheese, you're in for a whole new kind of corn bread!

1 cup yellow cornmeal
1 cup all-purpose flour
1/2 cup (2 ounces) shredded Monterey Jack cheese
1/4 cup sugar
2 tablespoons minced green bell pepper
2 tablespoons minced red bell pepper
2 teaspoons baking powder
1 1/2 teaspoons salt
1 cup (8 ounces) sour cream
2 eggs
1/4 cup (1/2 stick) butter, melted

Preheat the oven to 425°F. In a large bowl, combine the cornmeal, flour, cheese, sugar, bell peppers, baking powder, and salt. In another large bowl, combine the sour cream, eggs, and butter. Add the cornmeal mixture and mix well. Pour into an 8-inch square baking pan that has been coated with nonstick vegetable spray. Bake for 25 to 30 minutes, or until light golden on top and a wooden toothpick inserted in the center comes out clean. Cool slightly, serve warm.

Pull-Apart Italian Bread

We all love to eat with our fingers, and here's a recipe that lets us do just that. Go ahead, what are you waiting for? Bake it so you can eat it!

1 large package (17.3 ounces) refrigerated buttermilk
biscuits (8 biscuits), cut into sixths
1 small package (10.8 ounces) refrigerated buttermilk
biscuits (8 biscuits), cut into sixths
2 teaspoons dried oregano
1 teaspoon dried basil
1/2 teaspoon garlic powder
1/2 teaspoon onion powder
1/2 teaspoon salt
1/4 teaspoon cayenne pepper
1 tablespoon butter, melted

Preheat the oven to 350°F. Place the biscuit pieces in a large bowl and add all the remaining ingredients except the butter. Toss until the biscuits are evenly coated. Add the melted butter and toss again. Place in a 5" × 9" loaf pan that has been coated with nonstick vegetable spray. Bake for 40 to 45 minutes, or until golden brown on top. Let cool for 10 minutes, then remove from the pan. Serve warm or cool.

NOTE: Perfect served with Spicy Chunky Pizza Sauce (page 15).

Easy Herbed Onion Bread

1 loaf

When you're looking for something to have with your pasta instead of the same old traditional Italian bread, here's one that's just perfect for dunking in sauce.

2 tablespoons butter
1 large onion, finely chopped
(about 1½ cups)
3 cups biscuit baking mix
1 egg
1 cup milk
1 teaspoon dried basil
1 teaspoon dried dill

Preheat the oven to 350°F. In a large skillet, melt the butter over medium heat and sauté the onion for 5 to 7 minutes, or until tender. Meanwhile, combine the remaining ingredients in a large bowl. Add the onion to the bowl, mixing just until blended. Spoon into a 5" × 9" loaf pan that has been coated with nonstick vegetable spray. Bake for 55 to 60 minutes, or until golden on top. Let cool before removing from the pan.

Quick and Moist Bread

1 loaf

The secret to making this bread so moist is…well, I don't know if I should tell. See if you can find it yourself.

5 cups self-rising flour
$^1/_4$ cup plus 1 tablespoon sugar
1 tablespoon plus $^1/_2$ teaspoon
caraway seeds, divided
$1^1/_2$ cups (12 ounces) sour cream
1 can (12 ounces) lemon-lime soda
$^1/_2$ teaspoon coarse (kosher) salt
$1^1/_2$ teaspoons butter, melted

Preheat the oven to 350°F. In a large bowl, combine the flour and sugar. Stir in 1 tablespoon of the caraway seeds, then add the sour cream and soda alternately and mix well. Pour the batter into a 2-quart casserole dish that has been coated with nonstick vegetable spray. Sprinkle with the remaining $^1/_2$ teaspoon caraway seeds and the coarse salt. Bake for 45 minutes. Remove from the oven and brush with the melted butter, then bake for 15 to 20 more minutes, or until a wooden toothpick inserted in the center comes out clean. Let cool slightly, then cut into squares or wedges and remove from the pan.

NOTE: Did you guess the secret? Yup, it's the lemon-lime soda!

Italian Bread

1 loaf

No fancy bread machines for me! Let me share a home-style Italian bread that you'll make over and over again. Sure, this may take a little longer than my other breads, but it sure is worth the wait!

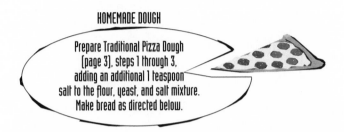

HOMEMADE DOUGH

Prepare Traditional Pizza Dough [page 3], steps 1 through 3, adding an additional 1 teaspoon salt to the flour, yeast, and salt mixture. Make bread as directed below.

Turn the dough onto a lightly floured board and form into a rectangle about 8" × 12". Starting at a 12-inch side, tightly roll up the dough jelly-roll fashion and place seam side down on an ungreased cookie sheet. Cover with plastic wrap and let rise at room temperature for 30 minutes until doubled in size. Preheat the oven to 400°F. Bake for 30 to 35 minutes, or until golden brown. Let cool, then cut into slices, or use as the base for a pizza or bruschetta.

Classic Bruschetta

8 to 10 slices

Tell your friends you're serving bruschetta and they'll look at you funny. But watch their faces change once they take their first bites!

1 loaf (12 to 16 ounces) Italian
bread, cut in half lengthwise
1/3 cup olive oil
1/4 cup plus 2 tablespoons chopped
fresh basil or 2 tablespoons dried basil
1 1/2 teaspoons salt
1 teaspoon pepper
10 medium-sized plum tomatoes,
seeded and chopped (about 4 cups)

Preheat the broiler. Place the bread cut side up on a cookie sheet and broil for 2 to 3 minutes, or until golden. Place on a large serving platter. In a large bowl, combine the remaining ingredients and mix until well blended. Spoon over the toasted bread. Cut and serve.

NOTE: *Mama mia!* Classic bruschetta is served with the topping either chilled or at room temperature. If you want your topping hot, return the bread to the oven after spooning the tomato mixture over it and broil for 2 to 3 more minutes, or until the topping is heated through.

Tomatoes!
Olive oil!
Basil!
A true
classic!

ITALIAN
BREAD

Pesto Bruschetta

Wow! If you love pesto as much as I do, you're going to want to make this bread every time you serve Italian food. And if you start with bottled pesto sauce, it takes no time at all.

1 loaf (12 to 16 ounces) Italian bread, cut in half lengthwise
1/3 cup Homemade Pesto Sauce (page 18) or prepared pesto
5 medium-sized plum tomatoes, sliced crosswise into 1/4-inch slices
1 cup grated Parmesan cheese

Preheat the broiler. Place the bread cut side up on a cookie sheet and broil for 2 to 3 minutes, or until golden. Remove from the oven and brush evenly with the pesto sauce. Layer the tomato slices over the sauce, then top with the cheese. Return to the oven and broil for 3 to 5 more minutes, or until the edges of the bread are golden brown. Cut and serve.

Mushroom and Swiss Bruschetta

12 to 14 slices

This is a great appetizer that's perfect with salad or even as a snack. Mmm!

1 loaf (12 to 16 ounces) French bread,
sliced diagonally into 12 to 14 slices
2 tablespoons vegetable oil
2 teaspoons chopped garlic (2 cloves)
3 cups sliced mushrooms (about 8 ounces)
$1/4$ teaspoon salt
$1/8$ teaspoon pepper
$3/4$ cup (3 ounces) shredded Swiss cheese

Preheat the broiler. Place the bread slices on a cookie sheet and broil for 2 to 3 minutes, or until golden. Remove from the broiler and set aside. (Leave the broiler on.) In a large skillet, heat the oil over medium heat and sauté the garlic for 1 minute, or until lightly browned. Add the mushrooms, salt, and pepper and sauté for 3 to 5 minutes, or until the mushrooms are tender. Spoon the mushroom mixture evenly over the bread, then sprinkle with the cheese. Return to the broiler for 2 to 3 minutes, or until the cheese is melted.

Mediterranean Bruschetta

12 to 14 slices

A little French bread, a little Fontina cheese, and this bruschetta is a true Mediterranean treat.

1 loaf (12 to 16 ounces) French bread,
sliced diagonally into 12 to 14 slices
¼ cup plus 3 tablespoons olive oil, divided
2 tablespoons fresh lemon juice
1 teaspoon ground cumin
1 teaspoon salt
½ teaspoon pepper
1 medium-sized eggplant (about 1 pound),
peeled, cut lengthwise in half, and then
crosswise into ⅛-inch slices
1 cup (4 ounces) shredded Fontina cheese

Preheat the broiler. Place the bread slices on a cookie sheet and broil for 2 to 3 minutes, or until golden. Remove from the broiler and reduce the oven temperature to 450°F. (Or preheat your oven to 450°F. if separate from the broiler.) In a medium-sized bowl, combine ¼ cup of the olive oil, the lemon juice, cumin, salt, and pepper; mix until blended. Add the eggplant and toss to coat. Lay the slices on a cookie sheet that has been coated with nonstick vegetable spray. Bake for 20 to 25 minutes, until the eggplant is tender. Remove from the oven and brush the toasted bread slices evenly with the remaining 3 tablespoons olive oil. Layer the eggplant evenly over the bread, then top with the cheese. Return to the oven and bake for 3 to 5 more minutes, or until the cheese has melted and the edges of the bread are golden brown. Serve immediately.

Herb Focaccia

6 to 8 servings

I know that with the name focaccia, this may sound complicated. And until I made it myself, I would have thought that, too—but it's not!

Pizza dough of your choice:

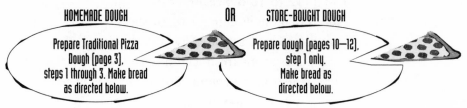

HOMEMADE DOUGH	OR	STORE-BOUGHT DOUGH
Prepare Traditional Pizza Dough (page 3), steps 1 through 3. Make bread as directed below.		Prepare dough (pages 10–12), step 1 only. Make bread as directed below.

2 tablespoons olive oil
1/2 teaspoon dried oregano
1/2 teaspoon basil

1/2 teaspoon dried minced garlic
1/8 teaspoon salt

Preheat the oven to 450°F. Using your fingertips or the heel of your hand, spread the dough to cover the bottom of a 10" × 15" rimmed cookie sheet that has been coated with nonstick vegetable spray. Prick the dough several times with a fork or paring knife and brush with the oil. In a small bowl, combine the remaining ingredients and sprinkle over the dough. Bake for 8 to 10 minutes, or until the crust is crisp and brown. Cut and serve.

Focaccia with Green Olives

6 to 8 servings

Focaccia is a dimpled Italian flat bread that is a "cousin" of pizza. It sure is gaining popularity today, so with just a few ingredients, why not enjoy another special family treat?

Pizza dough of your choice:

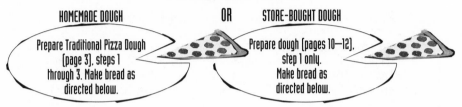

HOMEMADE DOUGH

Prepare Traditional Pizza Dough (page 3), steps 1 through 3. Make bread as directed below.

OR

STORE-BOUGHT DOUGH

Prepare dough (pages 10–12), step 1 only. Make bread as directed below.

1 cup sliced pimiento-stuffed green olives, drained

2 tablespoons olive oil

Preheat the oven to 450°F. Using your fingertips or the heel of your hand, spread the dough to cover the bottom a 10" × 15" rimmed cookie sheet that has been coated with nonstick vegetable spray. Prick the dough several times with a fork or paring knife and brush with the oil. Press the olive slices into the dough. Bake for 18 to 20 minutes, or until the focaccia is crisp and brown. Cut and serve.

Onion Focaccia

6 to 8 servings

Now this is one that'll bring back memories of your grandmother's cooking. It's old-fashioned–tasting, but with these doughs, it's today-style easy!

Pizza dough of your choice:

HOMEMADE DOUGH   **OR**   **STORE-BOUGHT DOUGH**

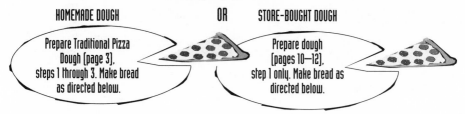

Prepare Traditional Pizza Dough [page 3], steps 1 through 3. Make bread as directed below.

Prepare dough [pages 10–12], step 1 only. Make bread as directed below.

2 tablespoons butter	1 egg, beaten
1 medium-sized onion, minced (about 1 cup)	1/2 teaspoon poppy seeds

Preheat the oven to 450°F. In a medium-sized skillet, melt the butter over medium heat and sauté the onion for 4 to 5 minutes, or until tender. Remove from the heat. Using your fingertips or the heel of your hand, spread the dough to cover the bottom of a 10" × 15" rimmed cookie sheet that has been coated with nonstick vegetable spray. Brush with the beaten egg, then spread the cooked onions evenly over the top. Sprinkle with the poppy seeds. Bake for 8 to 10 minutes, until the crust is crisp and brown. Cut and serve.

Sesame Parmesan Bread Sticks

16 bread sticks

These bread sticks are the perfect side dish for an Italian meal...why, they're perfect for *any* meal!

Pizza dough of your choice:

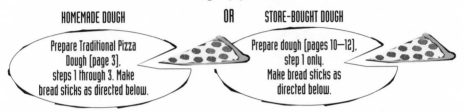

HOMEMADE DOUGH	OR	STORE-BOUGHT DOUGH
Prepare Traditional Pizza Dough [page 3], steps 1 through 3. Make bread sticks as directed below.		Prepare dough [pages 10–12], step 1 only. Make bread sticks as directed below.

¼ cup olive oil
¼ cup plus 2 tablespoons grated Parmesan cheese

¼ cup sesame seeds
2 tablespoons all-purpose flour

Preheat the oven to 450°F. Pour the oil into a 9" × 13" glass baking dish. In another 9" × 13" glass baking dish, combine the cheese and sesame seeds; set aside. Divide the dough into 16 pieces and shape each piece into a ball. With lightly floured hands, roll each ball into a rope about 12 inches long. Dip each rope in the oil, then into the sesame seed mixture, coating evenly. Gently twist each rope several times to create a spiraled look, then lay the bread sticks about 2 inches apart on 2 cookie sheets that have been coated with nonstick vegetable spray. Bake for 10 to 12 minutes, or until crisp and golden brown.

Tangy Bread Sticks

16 bread sticks

Wanna serve bread sticks with your meal, but tired of the same old store-bought bread sticks? Try these. They'll add zing to whatever you're serving.

2¼ to 2⅔ cups all-purpose flour, divided
1 package (¼ ounce) active dry yeast
1 teaspoon dried oregano
1 teaspoon salt
1 cup warm water
1 teaspoon sugar
½ teaspoon hot pepper sauce
1 tablespoon olive oil, divided
1 tablespoon caraway seeds
1 teaspoon coarse (kosher) salt

Place 2¼ cups flour, the yeast, oregano, and salt in a food processor. Pulse for 3 to 5 seconds, or until the ingredients are well mixed. In a small bowl, combine the water, sugar, hot pepper sauce, and 2 teaspoons of the oil. With the processor running, slowly pour the water mixture through the feeding tube. If the dough is too soft, add the remaining flour 1 tablespoon at a time until it forms a smooth ball. Add the caraway seeds and process for 20 seconds. Place the dough in a bowl that has been coated with nonstick vegetable spray and cover with plastic wrap; turn to coat. Let rise for 35 to 40 minutes, or until doubled in size. Preheat the oven to 450°F. Divide the dough into 16 pieces and shape each piece into a ball. With lightly floured hands, roll each ball into a rope about 12 inches long. Lay 2 inches apart on 2 cookie sheets that have been coated with nonstick vegetable spray. Brush the remaining 1 teaspoon oil over the bread sticks and sprinkle with the coarse salt. Bake for 10 to 12 minutes, or until golden brown.

Flavored Butters

Flavored butters are great for spreading on breads and rolls, and they're such a clever way to add more taste to your cooking, too. Don't be afraid to try them all.

Start each with ¹/₂ cup (1 stick) softened butter in a medium-sized bowl:

Dill Butter: Add 1 tablespoon chopped fresh dill or 1 teaspoon dried dill to the butter and mix by hand or with an electric beater until thoroughly combined. Use immediately, or cover and chill until ready to use.

Lemon Garlic Butter: Add 2 teaspoons garlic powder and 2 teaspoons lemon juice to the butter and mix by hand or with an electric beater until thoroughly combined. Use immediately, or cover and chill until ready to use.

Pesto Butter: Add 3 tablespoons Homemade Pesto Sauce (page 18) or prepared pesto to the butter and mix by hand or with an electric beater until thoroughly combined. Use immediately, or cover and chill until ready to use.

Roasted Garlic and Shallot Butter: Add the cloves from 1 bulb Roasted Garlic (page 19) and 1 teaspoon chopped shallots to the butter and mix by hand or with an electric beater until thoroughly combined. Use immediately, or cover and chill until ready to use.

Flavored Oils

Lots of gourmet stores and import stores carry flavored oils, and boy, are they pricey! Now you can have their homemade goodness at a fraction of the cost.

*Start each by placing 1 cup olive oil in a small jar
with a tight-fitting lid:*

Tarragon Oil: Add 6 sprigs fresh tarragon to the olive oil. Close the jar tightly and store for at least a week in a cool dark place, or until ready to use. This will keep for several weeks stored in the tightly sealed jar in a cool place.

Herbed Oil: Add 4 sprigs fresh oregano and 4 sprigs fresh basil to the olive oil. Close the jar tightly and store for at least a week in a cool dark place, or until ready to use. This will keep for several weeks stored in the tightly sealed jar in a cool place.

Hot Pepper Oil: Add 2 tablespoons crushed red pepper to the olive oil. Close the jar tightly and store for at least a week in a cool dark place, or until ready to use. This will keep for several weeks stored in the tightly sealed jar in a cool place.

NOTE: As time goes on, the flavor of the oil is enhanced, so make these in advance and keep them in your pantry until ready to use. You can use any of these flavored olive oils in place of regular olive oil in any of the recipes in this book (and in most others, too).

Dessert Pizzas

Stuck for what to make for a shower, office party, holiday dessert, or tonight's sweet snack? Why, pizza, of course! Sure, dessert pizzas will fit almost any occasion. And they're real attention-grabbers, too.

Your biggest problem is going to be what to make first. From Black Forest Pizza (page 181) and Strawberry Cheesecake Pizza (page 188) to Turtle Pizza (page 184), these are desserts that'll bring 'em running.

Surprised to find a whole chapter devoted to dessert? Most people will be. But after you sample these tempting sweet pizzas, I think you'll be devoted to surprising everyone you know with dessert pizzas!

Dessert Pizzas

Fruity Pizza

12 slices

This pizza is so colorful you're gonna need your sunglasses! Oh—the taste is just as colorful.

2 cups all-purpose flour
1 cup (2 sticks) butter, softened
1½ cups confectioners' sugar, divided
1 package (8 ounces) cream cheese, softened
1 teaspoon vanilla extract
1 container (8 ounces) frozen whipped topping, thawed
1 pint fresh strawberries, cleaned, hulled, and sliced
2 kiwis, peeled and sliced ½ inch thick
1 can (11 ounces) mandarin orange
pieces, drained and patted dry

Preheat the oven to 350°F. In a medium-sized bowl, combine the flour, butter, and ½ cup of the confectioners' sugar and, using your fingertips or the heel of your hand, spread the dough over the bottom of a 12-inch rimmed pizza pan that has been coated with non-stick baking spray. Bake for 20 to 25 minutes, or until golden; let cool. In a large bowl, with an electric beater, beat the cream cheese, the remaining 1 cup confectioners' sugar and the vanilla; mix well. Fold in the whipped topping. Spread over the cooled crust, then arrange the strawberries, kiwis, and oranges in a decorative pattern on top. Cover and chill for 2 hours before serving.

NOTE: You can use blueberries, peaches, nectarines, or almost any in-season fruit by itself or in combination. This will keep for several days covered in the refrigerator.

Cookie Pizza

16 slices

There is one drawback to this cookie treat—it won't fit in the cookie jar! I guess that won't matter, 'cause after your gang tastes it, there won't be any left to put away.

1/2 cup firmly packed light or dark brown sugar
1/4 cup granulated sugar
1/2 cup (1 stick) butter, softened
1 egg
1 teaspoon vanilla extract
1 1/4 cups all-purpose flour
1/2 teaspoon baking soda
1 small package (6 ounces) semisweet chocolate chips
1 can (16 ounces) white frosting
1/4 cup chopped walnuts
1/4 cup flaked coconut, toasted
1/4 cup colored-candy-coated chocolate candies

Preheat the oven to 350°F. In a large bowl, beat the sugars, butter, egg, and vanilla until creamy. Add the flour and baking soda; mix well. (The dough will be stiff.) Stir in the chocolate chips. Spread the dough over the bottom of an ungreased 12-inch pizza pan. Bake for 12 to 15 minutes, or until golden; allow to cool completely. Spread the frosting over the cooled cookie base, leaving a 1/4-inch border around the edge. Sprinkle with the walnuts, coconut, and candies. Cut into wedges and serve.

NOTE: You can top this dessert pizza with almost any of your favorite toppings. There are no rules! Why, you could even decorate it with jelly beans in your favorite team colors!

Fried Dough Pizza

10 to 12 slices

I must confess, this pizza isn't really fried at all, but it has the taste of our favorite fried dough dipped in cinnamon sugar. Mmm!

Pizza dough of your choice:

HOMEMADE DOUGH   **OR**   **STORE-BOUGHT DOUGH**

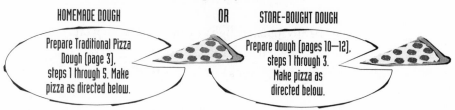

Prepare Traditional Pizza Dough (page 3), steps 1 through 5. Make pizza as directed below.

Prepare dough (pages 10–12), steps 1 through 3. Make pizza as directed below.

¹/₂ cup (1 stick) butter, melted, divided

2 teaspoons ground cinnamon

¹/₄ cup sugar

Preheat the oven to 450°F. Use a pastry brush to coat a 12-inch pizza pan generously with 2 tablespoons of the butter. Slide the dough onto the pan and flute the edges with your fingers. Brush the dough with 3 tablespoons of the remaining butter. Bake for 9 to 10 minutes, or until golden. Meanwhile, in a small bowl, combine the cinnamon and sugar; mix well. Remove the crust from the oven and, with the pastry brush, evenly distribute the melted butter on the top of the crust. Sprinkle half of the cinnamon-sugar mixture evenly over the top of the crust. Flip the crust over, brush with the remaining butter, and sprinkle evenly with the remaining cinnamon-sugar mixture. Flip the crust back over onto a serving plate. Cut and serve.

Rocky Road Pizza

12 slices

Years ago, when someone said there was a rocky road ahead, it meant that things were going to be rough. Well, things sure have changed—now we can look forward to a rocky road...a Rocky Road Pizza, I mean!

1 package (19.8 ounces) brownie mix
1 jar (7 ounces) marshmallow creme
$1/2$ cup semisweet chocolate chips
$1/2$ cup chopped walnuts

Preheat the oven to 350°F. Prepare the brownie mix according to the package directions and spread the batter evenly over the bottom of a 12-inch rimmed pizza pan that has been coated with nonstick baking spray. Bake for 22 to 25 minutes, or until a wooden toothpick inserted in the center comes out clean; let cool. With a wet table knife, spread the marshmallow creme evenly over the brownie pizza. Sprinkle with the chocolate chips and walnuts. Cut and serve.

Piña Colada Pizza

10 to 12 slices

You usually need a straw to enjoy piña coladas. Well, not this time!

Pizza dough of your choice:

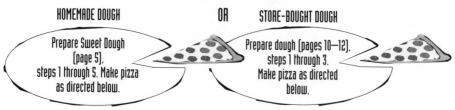

HOMEMADE DOUGH

Prepare Sweet Dough
(page 5),
steps 1 through 5. Make pizza
as directed below.

OR

STORE-BOUGHT DOUGH

Prepare dough (pages 10–12),
steps 1 through 3.
Make pizza as directed
below.

1 tablespoon butter, melted
1/2 cup pineapple preserves

1/4 cup sour cream
1/2 cup shredded coconut

Preheat the oven to 450°F. Brush the prepared dough with the butter and bake for 8 to 10 minutes, just until golden. Remove from the oven and set aside. In a small bowl, combine the pineapple preserves and sour cream. Spread over the top of the prepared crust, then sprinkle with the coconut. Bake for 6 to 8 more minutes, or until the coconut begins to brown. Remove from the oven and let cool to room temperature. Cut and serve.

Black Forest Pizza

From the Black Forest to the redwood forest and even Sherwood Forest—this is a taste loved around the world!

1 package (19.8 ounces) brownie mix
1 package (8 ounces) cream cheese, softened
2 tablespoons confectioners' sugar
1 container (8 ounces) frozen whipped topping, thawed
1 can (20 ounces) cherry pie filling

Preheat the oven to 350°F. Prepare the brownie mix according to the package directions and spread the batter evenly over the bottom of a 12-inch rimmed pizza pan that has been coated with nonstick baking spray. Bake for 22 to 25 minutes, or until a wooden toothpick inserted in the center comes out clean; let cool. In a large bowl, beat the cream cheese, confectioners' sugar, and whipped topping until smooth. With a wet table knife, spread the mixture evenly over the brownie pizza, then spoon the cherry pie filling evenly over that. Cut and serve immediately, or cover and chill until ready to serve.

French Brie and Walnut Pizza

10 to 12 slices

This pizza has such a rich and extravagant taste that your friends will think you paid lots of money for it at a fancy French bakery.

1 sheet (from a 17.25-ounce package) frozen puff pastry, thawed
$^1/_3$ cup raspberry preserves
1 small wheel (4$^1/_2$ ounces) Brie cheese, cut into 16 wedges
$^1/_4$ cup coarsely chopped walnuts

Preheat the oven to 400°F. With a rolling pin, roll out the pastry dough to fit a 12-inch pizza pan. Place the dough on the pan and pinch the edges down. Bake for 8 to 10 minutes, or until golden and puffy. Remove from the oven and reduce the oven temperature to 300°F. Using a second pizza pan or a cookie sheet, press down lightly on the puff pastry to flatten it slightly. Spread the raspberry preserves evenly over the crust, then arrange the Brie wedges over the top. Sprinkle with the walnuts and bake for 10 to 12 more minutes, until the cheese begins to melt. Cut and serve.

Apple Crumb Pizza

10 to 12 slices

I hope Grandma won't get mad when she finds out how easy this is to prepare—I mean there's no rolling pin and no apples to peel, yet the taste is so close to her deep-dish apple crumb pie!

1 refrigerated pie crust (from a 15-ounce package),
at room temperature
1 can (21 ounces) apple pie filling
1 cup all-purpose flour
1/2 cup sugar
1/2 cup (1 stick) butter, softened

Preheat the oven to 450°F. Place the pie crust on a 12-inch pizza pan that has been coated with nonstick baking spray. Use a fork to prick the dough several times; spread the apple pie filling over the top. In a medium-sized bowl, mix the remaining ingredients with a fork or pastry knife until crumbly. Sprinkle the flour mixture over the apple pie filling. Bake for 12 to 15 minutes, or until the crust and topping are golden brown. Cut and serve.

NOTE: Refrigerated pie crust can be found alongside the refrigerated doughs in the supermarket. They're so simple to use—just unfold and bake.

Turtle Pizza

10 to 12 slices

Boy, do I look forward to the holidays. Why? Because I have a friend who always gives me a great big box of turtle candies. Now that I have this recipe, I can have one of my favorite treats any time of year!

$^{1}/_{2}$ cup firmly packed light brown sugar
$^{1}/_{4}$ cup granulated sugar
$^{1}/_{2}$ cup (1 stick) butter, softened
1 egg
1 teaspoon vanilla extract
$1^{1}/_{4}$ cups all-purpose flour
$^{1}/_{2}$ teaspoon baking soda
1 small package (6 ounces) semisweet
chocolate chips
$^{3}/_{4}$ cup chopped pecans
$^{1}/_{3}$ cup caramel-flavored topping

Preheat the oven to 350°F. In a large bowl, with an electric beater, beat the sugars, butter, egg, and vanilla until creamy. Beat the flour and baking soda until well blended. (The dough will be stiff.) Stir in the chocolate chips until well combined. Using your fingers, spread the dough into a thin layer over the bottom of a 12-inch pizza pan that has been coated with nonstick baking spray. Sprinkle the pecans over the top and press lightly into the dough. Bake for 12 to 15 minutes, or until golden. Remove from the oven and drizzle with the caramel. Let cool, then cut and serve.

Blueberry Cheesecake Pizza

12 slices

When blueberries are in season, we want to eat as many as we can, but we can only make so many blueberry waffles and muffins! This is a great new way to enjoy fresh blueberries when they're in season, and everybody will be asking you, "How'd you think of that?"

1 package (20 ounces) refrigerated sugar cookie
dough, sliced 1 inch thick
1 package (8 ounces) cream cheese, softened
$^1/_3$ cup confectioners' sugar
1 pint fresh blueberries, rinsed and patted dry

Preheat the oven to 350°F. Place the slices of cookie dough on a 12-inch pizza pan that has been coated with nonstick baking spray. With lightly floured hands, press the dough together, forming 1 large cookie the size of the pan. Bake for 9 to 11 minutes, or until the top is lightly browned. Remove from the oven and let cool. Meanwhile, in a medium-sized bowl, with an electric beater on high speed, beat together the cream cheese and confectioners' sugar for 3 to 5 minutes, or until fluffy. Spread the cream cheese mixture over the cooled cookie dough, then top with the blueberries. Cut and serve, or cover and chill until ready to use.

NOTE: Until blueberry season, we can enjoy these same tastes by using a 21-ounce can of blueberry pie filling.

Peanut Butter–Chocolate Pizza

12 to 16 slices

This is just like having a GIANT chocolate-and-peanut-butter candy. It's a good thing I like to share, 'cause that makes it really fun to eat!

1 cup creamy peanut butter
1 cup (2 sticks) butter, melted
1 1/2 cups graham cracker crumbs
2 cups confectioners' sugar
1 package (12 ounces) semisweet
chocolate chips, melted
1/4 cup chopped salted or unsalted peanuts
1/2 cup puffed rice cereal

In a large bowl, combine the peanut butter, butter, graham cracker crumbs, and confectioners' sugar; mix well with a wooden spoon. Press the mixture evenly over the bottom of a 12-inch pizza pan that has been coated with nonstick baking spray. Pour the melted chocolate evenly over the top, then sprinkle with the peanuts and cereal. Cover and chill for 15 minutes. Slice and serve immediately, or cover and chill until ready to use.

Banana-Bread Pizza

12 to 16 slices

My family always loved spreading cream cheese on our banana bread—but that was a problem, because the bread always broke apart. *This* one doesn't!

1 cup granulated sugar
$^1/_2$ cup vegetable shortening
2 eggs
1 teaspoon baking soda
2 cups all-purpose flour
$^1/_2$ teaspoon salt
1 cup mashed ripe bananas
(about 3 medium-sized bananas)
1 teaspoon vanilla extract
$^1/_2$ cup chopped walnuts
2 packages (8 ounces each) cream cheese, softened
1 teaspoon confectioners' sugar

Preheat the oven to 350°F. In a large bowl, with an electric beater, cream together the granulated sugar and shortening until light and fluffy. Add the eggs and beat thoroughly. Gradually blend in the baking soda, flour, and salt. Beat in the mashed bananas and vanilla until smooth. Fold in the chopped walnuts. Spread the mixture onto two 12-inch pizza pans that have been coated with nonstick baking spray. Bake for 12 to 15 minutes, or until a wooden toothpick inserted in the center comes out clean. Let cool for 15 minutes. In a medium-sized bowl, beat the cream cheese until fluffy. Spread evenly over the top of 1 crust. Place the second crust, top side down, over the cream cheese. Sprinkle with the confectioners' sugar, and serve, or cover and chill until ready to serve, then sprinkle with the confectioners' sugar and cut.

Strawberry Cheesecake Pizza

12 to 16 slices

Okay, I admit it. I *love* strawberry cheesecake. I mean, who doesn't love its creamy, delicious texture and those sweet, crunchy, bright-colored strawberries? In fact, just thinking about it makes me want to go right into the kitchen so I can make this quick version!

1½ cups graham cracker crumbs
⅓ cup plus 2 tablespoons sugar, divided
½ teaspoon ground cinnamon
¼ cup (½ stick) butter, melted
1 package (8 ounces) cream cheese, softened
¼ cup sour cream
1 egg
½ teaspoon vanilla extract
4 cups sliced fresh strawberries (about 1 quart)

Preheat the oven to 350°F. In a small bowl, combine the graham cracker crumbs, 2 tablespoons of the sugar, and the cinnamon; mix until well blended. Add the butter and mix until blended. Press evenly over the bottom of a 12-inch pizza pan that has been coated with nonstick baking spray; set aside. In a large bowl, with an electric beater, beat the cream cheese, sour cream, egg, vanilla, and the remaining ⅓ cup sugar for 2 to 3 minutes, or until smooth. Spread evenly over the graham cracker crust, being careful not to lift the crust out of the pan. Bake for 20 to 22 minutes, or until the top is firm but not brown; allow to cool completely. Place the strawberries over the top. Cover and chill for 1 to 2 hours, then slice and serve.

Lemon Meringue Pizza

12 to 16 slices

Have you ever seen the beautiful lemon meringue pies bulging from the bakery counters in delis and diners? Well, this may not be as thick, but it's just as packed with flavorful, rich lemon filling and topped with a mountain of meringue.

2 cups all-purpose flour
1 cup (2 sticks) butter, softened
1/2 cup confectioners' sugar
1 package (3 ounces) lemon pie filling
3/4 cup granulated sugar, divided
2 1/4 cups water
2 egg yolks, beaten
4 egg whites
1/2 teaspoon cream of tartar

Preheat the oven to 350°F. In a medium-sized bowl, combine the flour, butter, and confectioners' sugar and use your hands to make a stiff dough. Spread the dough evenly over the bottom of a 12-inch pizza pan that has been coated with nonstick baking spray. Bake for 20 to 25 minutes, or until golden. Remove from the oven. Meanwhile, in a medium-sized saucepan, combine the lemon filling with 1/2 cup of the granulated sugar. Gradually stir in the water and the beaten egg yolks. Cook over medium-high heat, stirring constantly, for 4 to 5 minutes, or until the mixture comes to a boil. Pour onto the prepared crust and set aside. In a medium-sized bowl, with an electric beater, beat the 4 egg whites and the cream of tartar until foamy. Gradually add the remaining 1/4 cup sugar, and beat until stiff peaks form. Spread the meringue over the lemon filling, completely covering the crust. Bake for 4 to 6 minutes, or until the meringue is lightly browned. Cool until the filling is firm, then cover and chill for at least an hour before cutting and serving.

Index

A

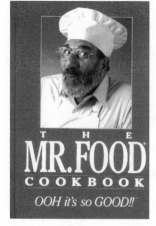

B

C

D

E

F

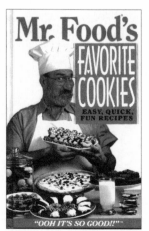

G

H

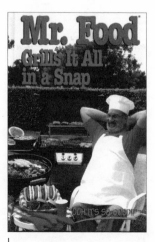

I

Mr. Food®'s Library Gives You More Ways to Say. . . "OOH IT'S SO GOOD!!™"

WILLIAM MORROW

J

K

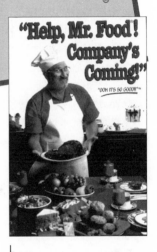

L

M

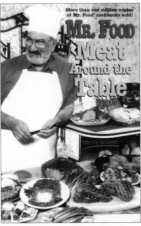

N

O

Mr. Food®

Can Help You Be A Kitchen Hero!

**Let Mr. Food® make your life easier with
Quick, No-Fuss Recipes and Helpful Kitchen Tips for**

**Family Dinners • Soups and Salads • Potluck Dishes
Barbecues • Special Brunches • Unbelievable Desserts**

. . . and that's just the beginning!

Complete your **Mr. Food®** cookbook library today.
It's so simple to share in all the
"OOH IT'S SO GOOD!!"™"

✂ -

TITLE	PRICE	QUANTITY	
A. **Mr. Food®** Cooks Like Mama	@ $12.95 each	x _____	= $_____
B. The **Mr. Food®** Cookbook, *OOH IT'S SO GOOD!!"*	@ $12.95 each	x _____	= $_____
C. **Mr. Food®** Cooks Chicken	@ $ 9.95 each	x _____	= $_____
D. **Mr. Food®** Cooks Pasta	@ $ 9.95 each	x _____	= $_____
E. **Mr. Food®** Makes Dessert	@ $ 9.95 each	x _____	= $_____
F. **Mr. Food®** Cooks Real American	@ $14.95 each	x _____	= $_____
G. **Mr. Food®'s** Favorite Cookies	@ $11.95 each	x _____	= $_____
H. **Mr. Food®'s** Quick and Easy Side Dishes	@ $11.95 each	x _____	= $_____
I. **Mr. Food®** Grills It All in a Snap	@ $11.95 each	x _____	= $_____
J. **Mr. Food®'s** Fun Kitchen Tips and Shortcuts (and Recipes, Too!)	@ $11.95 each	x _____	= $_____
K. **Mr. Food®'s** Old World Cooking Made Easy	@ $14.95 each	x _____	= $_____
L. "Help, **Mr. Food®**! Company's Coming!"	@ $14.95 each	x _____	= $_____
M. **Mr. Food®** Pizza 1-2-3	@ $12.00 each	x _____	= $_____
N. **Mr. Food®** Meat Around the Table	@ $12.00 each	x _____	= $_____
O. **Mr. Food®** Simply Chocolate	@ $12.00 each	x _____	= $_____

Call 1-800-619-FOOD (3663) or send payment to:
Mr. Food®

**P.O. Box 696
Holmes, PA 19043**

Name _____

Street _____ Apt._____

City _____ State_____ Zip_____

Method of Payment: ☐ Check or Money Order Enclosed

☐ Credit Card: ☐ Visa ☐ MasterCard Expiration Date _____

Signature _____

Book Total	$_____
+$2.95 Postage & Handling First Copy *AND* **$1 Ea. Add'l. Copy (Canadian Orders Add Add'l. $2.00 *Per Copy*)**	$_____
Subtotal	$_____
Less $1.00 per book if ordering 3 or more books with this order	$ –_____
Add Applicable Sales Tax (FL Residents Only)	$_____
Total in U.S. Funds	$_____

Account #: ☐☐☐☐☐☐☐☐☐☐☐☐☐☐☐☐☐

Please allow 4 to 6 weeks for delivery.   BKM1